Growing Up
MAD
in the *South*

Growing Up
MAD
in the *South*

Bonnie Henderson Schell

Edited by J.E. Harris, MA

ISBN print: 979-8-9868898-0-1

ISBN ebook: 979-8-9868898-1-8

Design and publishing assistance by The Happy Self-Publisher.

Flying Asylum Press

PERMISSIONS

Grateful acknowledgement is made for the use of the following either by permission or through the public domain.

"A Monster" is from "Being White in Atlanta during Desegregation," in *What Does It Mean to Be White in America? Breaking the White Code of Silence: A Collection of Personal Narratives*, ed. Gabrielle David and Sean Frederick Forbes, 2Leaf Press, 2016. University of Chicago Press. Used by permission."

"Scion of the Southland" by I. Granath. Georgia Tech Alma Mater. In the public domain.

"Bad" adapted from third person "B is for Bad," *Chinquapin* 9, Spring, 1988, University of California at Santa Cruz. Used by permission.

"Chocolate Dreams" revision, *Quarry West* 35, 1999, University of California at Santa Cruz. Used by permission.

"Do Lord, Oh Do Lord, Oh Do Remember Me" by author unknown. In the public domain.

"Give Me Oil in My Lamp" by author unknown. In the public domain.

"Glory, Glory," *WNC Woman: Women of the Spirit*, December 2014 Sandi Tomlin-Sutker, ed. Used by permission.

"God of the Marching Centuries" by D. P. McGreachy. Agnes Scott College hymn. In the public domain.

"Here We Go Loop de Loop" by author unknown. In the public domain.

"House" *North Carolina Bards Poetry Anthology 2022*. Local Gems Press.

"I'll Fly Away" by Albert Brumley. Used by permission.

"Interior McCain Library" provided by Agnes Scott College Archives and Special Collections. Used by permission.

Disclaimer about Language

"White Only" and "Colored" were my first spelling words. Those signs were above all the restrooms, water fountains, back doors to places, the streetcar, and the lunch counter in Woolworth's where my Granny took me for a grilled cheese. If you pulled ahead and started toward "Colored," someone, whether you knew them or not, would yell and yank you back until your arm hurt. I hope you won't mind that in some stories set in the 1950s, I have used the word "Colored" so that you will know how it was; however, I should tell you that I never heard a "colored" person call themselves that word.

Preface

In *Growing Up Mad in the South*, my characters drink buttermilk instead of mint juleps. They are small farmers, seamstresses, people who want to work for themselves, resilient, and eccentric survivors. In putting together this collection, I became aware of how the puzzlements of my childhood didn't go away. They are like strong sinews that bound muscle to growing bone and fragile facts to the neurons in my adult brain. To understand my family history, you must be able, as Samuel Taylor Coleridge wrote, to "suspend disbelief" and to believe that something isn't true is true in order to be convinced of something you need to be true:

To *believe* that my grandfather was a Holy Man.

To *believe* that my father died on Christmas Eve putting a tricycle together for me when I was three.

To *believe* that I have schizophrenia, which explains everything I experience.

To *believe* that God and Jesus love me even if they've never met me.

To *believe* that we are all created by God and in the image of God even though we will not share a meal of fried catfish and hush puppies with one another.

To *believe* that everyone who says "Bless Your Heart" cares about me and understands what has happened to me.

You cannot stop tiptoeing around, forcing them to confront the truth, without uncovering profound sorrow.

You can laugh about a mistaken belief, regret it, redeploy it, cry over it, curse it, save it for the future but never destroy it, even as it can destroy you and your children. Unless. Unless you can write a fiction better than Bible stories, history lessons, and campaign promises, that does not explain or blame.

Willingness to believe something that isn't true is necessary. To question it only brings about answers that fail to make anything better. The old questions, I found, have not and did not resolve, dissolve, or evolve. You have to live with them like hundreds of fireflies in the dark, spinning around your head, bobbing at your neck and arms, and making it hard to see what is ahead. Or coming from behind.

Table of Contents

Foreword

You have in your hands a rare and magical incantation of a book. I first met Bonnie in Asheville in 2016, when she signed up for my writing classes. Bonnie already had a long and varied background as a writer. For 30 years as a resident of California, she had published over twenty short stories, essays. and poetry, two newsletters, and Voices & Visions chapbooks presenting the voices of those who experienced madness and homelessness.

Although Bonnie was raised in the South, she had never written about the South until she moved back to North Carolina, or in other words, came home. Her voice is brave, ready, shocking, hilarious, poetic, and astute. Her writing shows a willingness for deep self-inquiry and casts a critical eye on society. She crawls into the taboo, the monstrous, and lifts up the tiniest detail we would have missed. Our mouths drop open and we gasp at the mastery it takes to bring alive these words and worlds.

Bonnie is one of my oldest students. Yet, while others may tire out, she persists. She possesses the courage to write into the nuances of psychic pain. Then, surprise! We find ourselves laughing. Bonnie's stories are rooted in simple things like small libraries, 3 by 5 cards, and potlikker. She captures the curiosity of a child searching for true and honest words, while running into withheld information and unexpressed family feelings. The result is a collection of work that is both grounded and utterly transcendent.

A rare and magical book indeed. May the whole world read it.

Nina Hart

Nina Hart is the founder of *Writing from the Top of Your Head* workshops and curriculum, and she is the author of *Somewhere in a Town You Never Knew Existed Somewhere.*

Words

Pale ladies with pink curlers hang over the top of the fence around our backyard, repeating nonsense syllables to me. They want me to stop crying.

"Wa da ya say, baby? Got a boo-boo? Coochie-coo. Lose your paci? Got a boo-boo? Wa da ya want to say, baby? Bye-bye. Say Bye-bye."

I am alone in my splintery wicker carriage under the magnolia tree for three hours every day. When I scream, I am developing my lungs because I was born too early because my parents got my egg from the buzzard's roost on top of Stone Mountain. Maybe it already had a crack in it. A lady baby doctor who prescribed my formula also ordered my abandonment in the backyard. It was important, she told my mother who told my Granny, not to pick me up if I cried.

Doctors and preachers give Mama a sad face as she tries to follow their orders. They are in charge of the words "must" and "ought," "should" and "have to." I see her going over instructions, repeating to herself what she must do. Then, she exclaims, "For God's sake!" Do my Mama and I have a sake?

Once I crawl to the bathroom closet behind a door where I find a blue box of white cardboard tubes filled with cotton and strings. I tear the paper off all of them, swing them in the air with the strings, make a humming whistle, and look through the tubes at my navel. I put a white tube in the corner of my mouth the way my uncle holds his cigarette. I arrange all the tubes in a circle around me. I am making fun.

When the door parts, I make a noise so they will know I am here behind the door and not mash me against the wall. I try to make a sound, but my throat holds my breath backwards until I say, "Bye-bye." My Aunt Willadeen holds my wrists too tight, yanks me off the floor, and throws me over the round Bendix washing machine. My mother gets the switches.

"This is going to hurt me worse than it hurts you," Mama says.

The machine is running. The drum is turning, the hot water swirling against my stomach. It could swoosh me off onto the floor or into the tub like one of Noah's animals fallen overboard, unnoticed for forty days and forty nights.

I am drowning, disappearing, but I can't cry while something that hurts is happening.

Uncle Judson comes to the door and pleads for them to stop. "She didn't know what she was doing," he says.

"She hid behind the door when the brains were passed out," Aunt Willadeen tells him.

When they stop, I slide my feet to the floor, my stinging legs wobbling, and I run away as fast as I can to curl up under my ABC quilt.

Granny teaches me the A, B, C's, and I learn to sing them.

"*ABCDEFG. HIJKLMNOP. QRS. TUV. WX. Y and Z. Now I know my A-B-C's. Tell me what you think of me,*" but no one does.

After I am too loud in the house, a bad girl, they will not talk to me. When I walk across the floor, no one sees me.

My Granny doesn't talk in front of them, but in our room, she tells me stories. She can read all the words in The Holy Bible. Starting at the beginning, she tells me about the first parents and their sons who fight until one is dead. I hear about David and

Goliath, Jonah beating on the ribs of the whale when no one could hear him, Moses standing too close to the Burning Bush, and Joseph with his coat of many colors that his Granny made. I know the command that says, "Suffer the little children." Those are some of the "wonderful words of life" parents sing in church.

Granny teaches me to spell. My daddy paints the beautiful letters of words on signs, but he is not home. This is my first spelling word:

"The B-i-b-l-e.

Yes, that's the book for me.

I stand alone

on the word of God,

the B-i-b-l-e."

There are three important books in the house–the telephone directory, the Sears catalog, and The Holy Bible. The Bible must always be on top so anyone can find it without searching. Granny sends me to get a book to stand on because she is making a dress for me and needs to mark and turn the hem. I bring The Holy Bible, put it in the seat of a chair, and climb up. Mama and my aunt come to the door.

"My Lord, look at her!" they say.

I think they see how I'm growing up so fast.

"She's standing on the promises of Christ the King." I am. Carefully, I have my feet placed perfectly side by side on the book that was written by a King named James. I stand as straight as a young pine tree. Where did my Granny go? I am alone. I know they have gone to get the switches, but I am not going to get down.

There are hundreds, thousands of words floating around the Earth, naming things. Everybody can catch the ones they need. But there is a rule about standing on the words that tell stories. You are not supposed to do it.

Bad

The house makes my throat choke. Aunt Willadeen collects straw flowers and stores them in brown plastic vases nailed to the facings of all the doors. My Granny and my Mama, who threw out the dry, dusty flowers when they were in our bedroom, never say anything to Aunt Willadeen because the house is hers. My dark, bitter, red asthma medicine is in the kitchen on the top shelf with a white prescription label on the bottle; it is the first place I saw my name typed – "Bonnie Jo Henderson--as needed."

When the chicken man and his family from Hartwell, Georgia, come to see Uncle Judson and Aunt Willadeen, Mama doesn't want me to stay in the living room near them. She tells them I'm allergic to their poultry, but Mama says their children have rickets and he can't write his own name. His name is Hubert Hart, and he comes on Saturdays in a Ford truck and blows the horn in the driveway. My mother says this is rude. Uncle Judson spends Saturdays listening to "The Red Silk Stockings and the Green Perfume" with my dead daddy's picture in his lap and a can of beer. But when Hubert Hart sounds his horn, Uncle Judson springs up and runs to the bottom of the driveway to help with the cocks.

The men stay out late on Saturday nights, and I know where they go because once, when my Aunt Willadeen and Mama had gone on a hospital visitation, Uncle Judson took me with him. We went outside of Smyrna to a tabernacle that had half-burned down in a baptizing service by candlelight. The enclosure was crowded with men in bright shirts with their hats pulled down low over their eyes and their money in little bags. Most had birds in small wire cages, but Mr. Hart carried his in a box.

"If they fight for air inside, they'll fight for blood outside," he told another farmer.

I remember the crowd backing out into a circle and cooing to the birds. I was on my uncle's shoulders, and I held my fists over my eyes when a beak pummeled the eye of a red bird. The cocks would jump on each other's backs and peck between the shoulder blades. Sometimes they would back away and display their feathers. Their combs were the color of raw liver. My uncle yelled at me to hold still just before the black cock squawked a broken cry and froze open-beaked, dying in the air. I never told my mother.

One particular Friday, the Harts come early to have lunch and buy their Easter clothes in Atlanta. My uncle is taking a nap. My mother is at work. I see Mr. Hart exit out the back door of the kitchen. Aunt Willadeen and Mrs. Hart are baking and I have nothing to do, so I follow the chicken man with my eyes but stay near the screened door at the top of the back stairs. He roams through an overgrown patch of black-eyed Susans at the end of the yard. He has long bones and big feet. His neck tilts out of his collar like a fishing pole with a round bobber on the end.

Turning his head with half-closed eyes, he sees me looking at him. Then he reaches out and snatches the black-eyed Susans off their stems. I do not move. When he turns his back to me, I close the screen door and slip back into the house.

"Don't you go out in the backyard when the chicken man is there," my Granny always says. "You hear me, Bonnie?"

Aunt Willadeen, Mrs. Hart, and the kids are grouping in the living room to leave. In the bedroom Granny is sitting up, adjusting her stomach in her corset. I wait for her to say something to me.

"What have you been doing, Bonnie?"

"Nothing, Granny," I answer, twisting and tying the tails of my blouse.

"Well, come here and get my soap from under the bed and wash yourself good. Your mama's coming early to get you so you can meet her new man friend. She wants you to be clean and well behaved. Now you go wash." Granny leans back on the bed and folds her arms across her chest. When she sleeps, she keeps her mouth open with her upper dental plate resting on her tongue.

I get the soap out of her box and go to the bathroom. I draw a basin, letting the water pulse through my fingers into the sink. I take off my blouse and my shorts and dip the soap in the water and rub it on my face. If Mama gets married, she says I might have piano lessons. I smear the bar of Ivory all over my chest and arms until I look as white as a ghost. My uncle's brown bar of Borax is in his soap dish. I wet it and glide it over the white soap on my face and stomach. While the soap is getting me clean, I brush my teeth and spit in the middle of the mound of foam in the sink. The last thing I do is take off my underpants, turn away from the mirror and wash my "privates."

When Granny helps my sister and me take a bath, she washes our ears and necks, checks our elbows and knees, and then tells us to turn around with our backs to her to wash between our legs. If God had taken longer than a week to make us, I think, He might have redone our "privates." Otherwise, we wouldn't have to hide those parts. Once, I was in a hurry to print the alphabet for Granny, and she said, "I'd be ashamed for people to see my work if it was that messy." Underwear is to keep God from being ashamed.

I splash water on all the soap and dry myself with a towel. Granny is asleep with her arms flung out flat on the bed, so I go in the closet where my family's clothes hang in the dark.

Next to Granny's coat is Mama's best silk dress that makes Granny pray when Mama puts it on. It has a swag of pleats across one hip. I once nestled a bird's fallen nest in the pouf to keep the baby birds safe, but mites got in the closet, ruined my Daddy's Navy uniform, and I got spanked.

When I go to tell Granny I am clean, she rolls over on her side and raises her head.

"Is that Hart man in the back yard? Don't I hear him singing?"

"I don't know, Granny."

"Well, you stay in the house and put on your good dress so you'll look like something."

"Yes, Granny. Yes, Granny," I whisper. She falls back on the bed with her wide palms on her head.

I have a white dress that is the most special thing that my Granny has made. It is organdy with embroidered roses and lace tatting scalloped around the pinafore. She measured me every day for a week with a tape line to make sure that it would fit, and then put in growing tucks to be let out. My sister can't stay still to get measured, but she doesn't like dresses anyway.

"I won't be here to make your wedding dress," she told me, "so I'll make you a white organdy." There were matching white pants with lace around the leg-holes and a slip with embroidered buttonholes.

I pull the dress off the hanger and the slip and pants out from under two clothespins. I tie the sashes, leaving the dress and the slip for Granny to button. She is still asleep with her feet hanging off the end of Mama's twin bed.

At the top of the back stairs, I hear the singing. Hubert Hart's voice is high and thin, and it makes a fluttering whistle as it slips through his throat up the long neck to his mouth. He is standing with cocks under his arms; the side of their heads pressed to his ribs so that they seem to listen to him with two single glistening eyes.

"Cock-a-bow, cock-a-bite, Cock-a-crow, cock-a-cite," he sings. "Cock-a-low, cock-a-lie, Cock-a-do, cock-a-die."

He squats down and holds them by the necks, pretending to let them go and then holding them back again. When he stands up, he kicks them under their necks. With his head flung back and his right hand over his head, he turns and turns in the sun, singing his song to the cocks, and kicking them in the throat.

"Cock-a-bow, cock-a-bite, cock-a-crow, cock-a-cite."

One cock darts at the other cock's face. The iridescent feathers spring out, and the cocks fly in the air dragging their feet over each other's backs. Mr. Hart's mouth is open and the long veins in his neck bulge. He swings his hand over his head. From the back porch, his hand looks gray. It moves at a slower rhythm than his head and his legs.

As soon as the cocks begin to screech and fight, Mr. Hart separates them, stroking their beaks and rubbing their heads.

"Cock-a-low, cock-a-lie, cock-a-do, cock-a-die."

He stuffs them in their boxes secured with a metal grating. His light brown hair hangs over his face and his long neck like the stringy tassels on an ear of corn. My father's hair was black and smooth like a panther's. Mr. Hart wears thick brown shoes. I wonder why he doesn't wear heavy gloves.

I turn back inside the house and go in the kitchen. It is time for my medicine. My dress is still unbuttoned. I try to reach the medicine but take down a glass instead and fill it with cold water. I keep one hand over the top of it, so the water won't spill, and walk carefully down the back steps. Mr. Hart doesn't look at me until I am behind him, and then he blinks over his shoulder.

"My Granny says to give you this water."

I hold up the glass to his face. The sun sparkles blue and yellow curves in the edges of the water. He takes the glass out of my hand. The water pours out the edges of his mouth and streams down the sides of his neck. He drops the glass in the shoots of wild Susans. Lines of water lay in the grooves of his hand. He holds it for me to see with his middle finger sticking out, pointing at my stomach, and the thumb and other fingers curled into his palm. I pick up the glass and back away, running up the back steps.

Back down at the bottom of the steps, I squat down before the fake lily pond. My Granny made the lilies out of crepe paper and then my uncle dipped them in thick wax so they would float. They are beautiful. I move the lilies around with my little finger.

A fat wasp sits on the edge of the cemented pond. My face in the pond is pale and still. My eyes follow the wasp. Spinning around my head, it makes a veil of gauzy air over my hair. The wasp lands on my neck and walks across the yoke of my dress, settling its legs in three picots of tatting. I look at him, at the polished black beads on the sides of his head. He drifts before my eyes and hovers, suspended, over my collar. I watch him the way I watch all things that are scary. I see him and me, still and whole, in a separate space. The thoughts in my head stop. I am waiting to be stung, but it won't hurt while I am watching.

An arm thrusts itself out over my head, snatches the wasp out of the air and throws it to the ground, breaking its wings. Hubert Hart leans over and slowly buttons up my slip and my dress. He stands behind me for a while with his legs pushing against my back. Then he climbs up the steps to the back door and sits down. I follow him and wait, facing him two steps below.

He spreads the skirt of my organdy dress over his knees and fingers the embroidery. Then he leans his head on his right arm against the banister. I can see the veins across the bones in his neck turn blue. His eyelashes are white on the ends and the sun makes a shadow of lines through them on his cheeks like fine scratches. The sides of his nose are so thin that I can see the air moving in and out of his head. His lips are chapped.

I touch the lines of his cheek with a timid hand, and he raises his fingers to my wrist to stop me.

He holds his left hand close to my eyes. It is the ugliest thing I have ever seen, but I don't make a face.

"You think it's ugly?" he asks. One of his fingers has been split in two. Scar tissue and calluses cover his palm.

I know I should say "No," but I can't. I ask him if it hurts because I think things that are ugly must cause pain. He turns the hand over and touches the roses. He moves his hands over my yoke until I feel the nipples on my chest tickle. He holds me by the neck and breathes on me. I think that he is the saddest man I have ever seen. He looks out across the patch of black-eyed Susans, scans the yard, and then looks over his shoulder at the back door.

He wets his rough lips with his tongue. His fingers stretch out to meet his thumb around my neck and my eyes begin to burn. The sides of his nose flare. His knees clamp against my thighs and make my stomach hurt. I know immediately, though minutes seem absent and gone, that I am going to die. He closes his eyes. He puts his fingers inside my underwear, stretching my Granny's lace. His hand is rough and it hurts. Inside me, he moves my stomach around like a puppet. I concentrate on waiting.

His face shudders. Then his head bobs and falls back like a burden too heavy. I cough.

His hand falls between his legs, and he holds on to himself, shaking. The sores made by the cocks are red like trails of fire ants.

Back in the house I go to our bedroom and touch Granny's forehead. She opens her wrinkled eyelids and stares at me.

"Well, don't you look pretty," she exclaims. I push the knot of my sash into my back with my hands and wait.

"Your Granny's not going to be able to keep you forever, Bonnie." I don't know that.

"Can I have my medicine now, Granny?" I beg, though my throat is open and clear, but dryer than the dead flowers. Granny hobbles into the kitchen and takes down the medicine. A spoonful is not enough. I swallow it slowly, making it last, a round bitter secret.

That night I start sleeping on my back so I can see who might be coming. Before that night, I always fell asleep on my stomach with one leg crossed over Granny's foot, one arm hanging off the edge of our mattress and the other arm propped on my pillow so I could suck my thumb. That night, a jolt strikes me between the shoulder blades and wakes me up. I turn over on my back and fall asleep again.

Then face up on my pillow I start to choke. The chicken man's breathe is on me, and his hand is around my throat.

Glory, Glory

In Atlanta, Georgia, my grandmother, Bonnie Belle Henderson, took me to hear a glory preacher, a speaker in tongues, and a prophetess. Missus Barth, under a tent, had a choir of angel singers.

It was forbidden ground. My Mama said I could not go.

Before we took the streetcar, Granny said to wash my feet because Missus Barth's disciples were going to purify us with Ivory in a basin. I carefully left the dirt between my toes.

The other angels were not as giant as my Granny who always held my hand crossing the street.
She could make big trucks stop.

From the wooden slatted chairs, I could see the light shining on Missus Barth, the glory woman preacher. Arms swayed high, begging, moving the holy air up over my fingers. Granny let go of my hand. And God forgot to breathe. The groaning ecstasy of stout saints sifted me down to the sawdust covered floor. They rose to shout Glory!

Glory, Glory, Glory

Glory. My Granny had forgotten me. Her eyes were fixed above.

I saved myself. I crawled to the aisle at the end of the row, found shelter under the grand piano at the edge of the tent. It was dark where I saved myself, like hiding under the bed waiting for the boogeyman. My white socks were dirty, lace torn.

Missus Barth laid on the altar and the angels unrolled their knots of hair, parted it loose, hairpins flying around like July sparklers under that sky grey tent where I lost my Granny to an angel army in August 1949.

Bite Your Tongue

The first thing I remember about my tongue is that I burnt it up. Atop the four-shelf bookcase that divided the kitchen from the front room sat a clay pot with a green plant covered in little red peppers. By standing on the living room side on a blue striped stool with curly rips, I could reach it. One day I climbed up, pointed, and touched one pepper.

"Pretty, pretty," I said, looking across at my Granny.

She said, "Hot, hot."

"Pretty, pretty," I repeated, hoping she would get the pot down for me.

"Hot," Granny said as she turned away, returning to the back porch to hang the damp kitchen towels. I went as high as my tip toes would go, and lickety-split, pulled off all the pretty red peppers I could reach and gobbled them up. A fire enveloped my mouth, and I began crying and yelling, sending Granny running towards me as I flailed my arms, then held my cheeks.

"What have you done, child? Did you eat those peppers?"

No. I shook my head from side to side, unable to speak.

All the candles of my birthday cake were ablaze under the roof of my mouth. My tongue felt as blistered as my arm did when I laid it across the hot oven rack. My tongue was a red balloon.

"Don't you lie to me!" she scolded. "Well, I'll show you what we have to do." I was still screaming and crying but Granny said, "Be quiet. You did it, so don't complain."

She got her bar of Ivory soap and a glass of water. Holding my head back by my hair, she rubbed the soap on the insides of my cheeks, over the surface of my tongue, and up over the roof of my mouth. Next, she made me drink some water to make soap suds.

"Swish it side to side," she said, "but don't swallow it. Spit it out."

I had already swallowed. Now my throat was on fire. I wrapped my fingers around it and screamed. Granny stuffed in sticks of butter and tablespoons of white lard until I could barely breathe, but the flames died down. It was two days and a night before I could eat something as gentle as applesauce and rice.

Sometimes, I heard big people say to bite your tongue, so I would try by smashing my teeth down in the middle of my tongue, and although I only had baby teeth, it still hurt. If Mama said that her sister didn't have the sense to come in out of the rain, Granny would tell Mama, "Bite your tongue." At first, I wondered why Granny would say such a mean thing, but she and Mama shared a half smile and nodded toward each other.

Words could be tricky I decided.

When my front baby teeth got loose, I wiggled them back and forth with my tongue. Mama wanted me to let Uncle Judson pull them out with pliers, but I covered my mouth, shook my head, and ran. Soon the two teeth hung by tiny red threads, which drove Mama crazy.

"You'll swallow those teeth and they'll cut up your insides," she warned, "and you will surely die."

I hoped she would bury me next to my father.

When those teeth finally fell out, I thought I would get two quarters if I put them under my pillow and kept my eyes closed, but Mama said I had been too "Obstinate." I didn't know what that word meant, but I felt the way it sounded: *Obstinate*. I probed the holes behind my upper lip with my tongue. In one, my tongue tip touched the sharp point of a new tooth coming up. I kept poking at it, and it grew up like a flower.

On Saturday nights, while Mama was brushing her hair over her forearm to turn it under and pinching her cheeks until they were rosy, she sent me into the living room to entertain suitors who had come to take her out on a date. I would say "Hello" and sit at one end of the couch across from the armchair where they always sat with their shiny toed shoes. If he didn't say anything, then what was I supposed to say? I felt tongue-tied.

"Cat got your tongue, missy?" a suiter once asked.

"Don't have a cat. I have a little turtle. She doesn't swim anymore."

"Oh... Do you want to hear a tongue twister?"

"Yes," I said even though I didn't.

"Peter Piper picked a peck of pickled peppers," he recited. "How many pecks of pickled peppers, did Peter Piper pick?"

"That rhyme's wrong, Mister," I told him. "Peppers don't come pickled. Somebody has to do it to them and who would want to because they're hot as fire. My family eats pickled peaches and watermelon pickles, and bread and butter pickles, which don't have a bit of bread in them. My uncle likes pickled pigs feet from a tall jar. Have you ever eaten pickled pigs feet?"

He scrunched up his eyes and stuck out his long tongue. It was coated in yellow which meant he had a sick stomach and needed a dose of castor oil.

"You should try them," I said. "Men like them." Then, without asking, I recited my own tongue twister. "Betty Botter bought some butter but, she said, this butter's bitter. If I put it in my batter-"

"*What*?" he interrupted.

"-it will make my batter bitter-"

"Hey kid, *stop!*"

"-but, a bit of better butter will make my batter better."

"So," he asked me, shaking his head, "do you bake cakes with your mother?"

"Never have. But I once had a mouthful of sticks of butter because I did something bad."

He didn't even ask me what I did. Instead, the man looked at his wristwatch, picked up his hat, and went out the front door before Mama even came in to see him. Mama looked so beautiful that I was glad he didn't see her. I knew I was in for a tongue lashing, but then my mind went blank about what I might have said. She put her hands on her hips and ordered me to repeat everything I said to him so I just started saying whatever I could think.

"He thought I had a cat and that you should bake cakes with me."

She covered her ears.

She put up the palms of her hands to my face.

"Enough. Hold your tongue."

I knew not to do that. She only wanted me to shut up because every bad thing that happened to us was my fault. I had caused my daddy to go away and me and Granny and my sister and Mama to have to live with my uncle and aunt where we were not welcome. Even when Mama was smiling for others, her eyes looked far away beyond me.

Bugs

When I was little,
I wanted bugs to like me,
to feel at home taking a stroll
up my chubby arms and neck.

To be party to their small communications,
to march and meet with them in the shade,
summoned by telepathic hellos.
I wanted to have their skill at escaping calamity,

to swing in camouflage on a web.
When big people tell children, "Shut up," over
and over, yell *"Don't talk back to me,"*
on the one hundredth time,

thunder over the continent
rattles all branches and ground.
Insects, spiders, and beetles come forth to whisper
into big hairy ears and those with pearl and rhinestone clips.

Big people stop a minute,
slap their ears to stop the tickle
as bugs whisper in unison, "Listen, listen, listen.
You. Listen." Big people push a thumb against the sound.

When it is safe, the bugs will crawl out,
lay their intricate segments and wounded wings
across my lap. Cumbersome, mouthy girl,
I keep them safe and hum them well.

Here We Go
Loop de Loop

My sister and I had matching twin beds with blue padded headboards and white frames with a stripe of gold. The room was small, so my bed was flush against the wall next to my parents' bedroom. For hours I would listen to them arguing, occasionally saying my name, and my mother telling my stepfather not to say, "God damn it." Later my mother would scream and whimper. Then they would be quiet.

When I can't go to sleep, I uncurl myself, stretch my legs and arms and ascend to the ceiling, pushing through to the grey asbestos roof. Up over my house, I fly forward over red brick ranch style homes on my street, then the next, and the next. I do not beat my arms like a bird; I float, dip down to see who is still up, sitting alone, or walking the hall on a scratched metal walker. Sometimes from above I find them reading intently while children lay at their feet on a ragged mattress. Sometimes from above I find them holding their heavy head in their hands, a gracefully shaped bottle next to them.

I lift up, moving higher to see warehouses, parking lots with concrete broken by weeds, lone police cars, the Ford dealership lit up like Christmas, and schools with the lights out. Landing back in my bed just happens and I bundle up because the outside night air is cold.

I can't stay out too long because if I am caught out of bed, my stepfather gets his belt with the initialed brass buckle. When I know he is coming, I refuse to cry or hide. I tried putting a book in my pants like Tom Sawyer, but it slipped out. I watch from the ceiling and when I see his thin, terse lips smile, I am scared, but the stinging and pain from the welts on my legs and buttocks no longer hurt. On Fridays he would beat me and my sister, saying we must have done something wrong during the week. My sister continued to yell but I would not give him the satisfaction.

It is possible to go around the world on a swing, to fly up and over. I have felt it. Every time I pump my legs, I swing back further and farther, my swing goes higher and higher, and my brown lace up shoes point straight up to the clouds. I know I can, I know that I can fly. Children can fly until an adult says we can't. I had a friend to swing with me, but one day her missionary parents to Africa took her out of class without telling me. They brought pink cupcakes with chocolate sprinkles for our whole class, gathered the trash and their daughter and went out the door for good. If I could go around the world on my swing, I might see her again.

"Here we go Loop de Loop, here we go Loop de Lie"

What if we many children could together go Loop de Loop at the same time? How grand that would be.

When people die in the country, neighbors gather in the Noah's Ark church. They don't hold heavy hymn books; they sing by heart, *"I'll fly away, Oh Lordy, I'll fly away. Like a bird from prison bars has flown, I'll fly away."*

Only my mother stands, staring into the coffin, clutching the cold fingers.

Me, little Granny, my mother's mother, and most of the church people sing, *"When I die, Hallelujah. Bye and bye, I'll fly away."*

And my big Granny, whom my stepfather allows to have a bed at our house, can do it.

She practices in her bed with her arms raised, ready to fly.

We both want to be free.

House

I draw a home, a square with a triangle top.
I keep bricks and a box lid folded
under my Mother Goose blanket, embroidered in squares.
Jack be nimble, jump to leap the flames.

My alphabets, rolled like scrolls, rest under the iron arm of my
    grandmother's oak domed Singer.
My dresses and leggings rest tucked under the bed
with Jeannie girl, Mama, me, then Granny.

Across the pitch of our hearts I lay, keeping watch. "Work for
    the night is coming when man's work is o'er,"
sings the preacher on the radio, and Granny answers "Surely,
surely, surely He meaneth me."

The square house belongs to Aunt Willadeen and Uncle Judson,
    the man my daddy told to love me. I stay in the back.
Not to touch Bibles, *Readers Digest*, and almanacs
leaning on their shelves with what-nots.

One by one, I take torn, mildewed books to read. Their voices
    rejoice with me.
"Bringing in the Sheaves," sneaking every word back
to the spaces absent dust. Be quick, Jack.

I learn "Yes Sir," "No Ma'am," "Don't talk at the table," so a
    stepfather will want me, sister, and Mama.
They all know where my father went,
the whys twisted from the rules that go back and forth.

"Look no dark man in the eye for he will stab you." "Keep your
    head up, don't squint or frown."
Then without stumbling, re-learn to walk.
I'm a clever, patient girl. They all say it.

Wheezing in that musty house, I learn to push sound around,
my tongue as resilient as a wet clapboard.

Chocolate Dreams

The ice cream man rang his bell for Hunkie bars.
Vanilla cream center coated
with dark chocolate sheets of ice.
Breaking off, falling to my skirt,

sliding down my arm, a blackened tongue.
"Oh, it's too rich," they said about chocolate.
"Chocolate will make you sick.
Take what the ice cream man hands you, but

don't you touch him. All day
his hands touch filthy coins.
He's so dirty nasty. Lord knows
where his heathen hands have been,

for he comes from an igloo in the slums."
They didn't know I sucked his change
before I washed my hands. Sweet pennies.
On the front porch, I tore the paper from my Hunkie bars.

Carefully lifted the crusts to drop
in a jar, collecting chocolate, waiting.
Waiting until I had enough to freeze
and eat my rich, dark delicious death.

Bang, Bang, You're Dead

Mr. Merritt brought his son William, who everyone called "Boomer," to see me every Saturday so we might get acquainted since we were the same age. Boomer arrived dressed in a complete Hopalong Cassidy outfit - black fringed shirt and pants, cowboy scarf, hat, chaps, pointed toe boots with spurs, and a holster with pistols and caps. The sound and smell of smoking cap pistols scared me as much as New Year's Eve sparklers or fireworks on the Fourth of July.

"Those firecrackers will blow the eyes right out of little boys and girls," my Granny claimed.

Hooking his thumbs in his belt, Boomer walked with a swagger. No matter what question I directed to him to start a conversation, he would ask in a long drawl, "So, who wants to know?" I was supposed to be nice to him, but that was hard.

As soon as Mr. Merritt and Boomer arrived, his son ran through the house to the backyard to hide. My mother would shake me from my reading and send me out to play. Mr. Merritt said I stayed indoors too much.

"All work and no play makes Jack a dull boy," he said.

"But I'm a girl," I replied. Clearly, this did not apply to girls, but he only stared at me.

Outside, I looked for Boomer behind bushes and sheds, or under the steps, until I got close enough for an ambush.

"Bang, bang! You're dead," he'd yell, leaping out at me, the quick, harsh sound of the caps rang in my ears and the sulfurous scent of the powder stung my nose. At first, to please him, I would fall down and play dead.

"I only wounded you, dumbbell!" he would holler, kicking me to get up and run so he could pursue me. Somebody must have called Boomer that word a lot because he sure liked to say it.

For my sister's birthday in July, Mr. Merritt bought a blue swing set. She loved the monkey bars and could hang upside down, sometimes from only one leg. I loved the swing so long as my feet could touch the ground. I didn't want anyone to push me from behind but preferred to pump myself up toward the sky. Boomer's goal was to go "round the world," to swing over the top steel bar. I knew that was impossible. Besides, the top of the swing set was not the center of the world, but Boomer made me push him until he was so high, he was above my head.

"Get out of my way, dumbbell!"

We had to eat tomato and mayonnaise sandwiches together on the back steps. During lunch, Boomer showed off his tricks - turning his eyelids inside out, curling his tongue up over his upper lip and folding his lower lip down, or blowing straws out of his nose. It seemed to me that cowboys want only to impress you, not to be a friend.

Sometimes, Boomer brought his toys to share, but I was not skilled at catching balls, throwing horseshoes, or aiming plastic balls at bowling pins, so my Granny bought us both jars of bubble blowing liquid and two wands. I delighted in making sparkling bubbles around my head. Just as the bubble reaches the right size, you pause, and wait before firmly sending it out on its own. Boomer tried it once and blew too hard, producing fragments.

"It doesn't work. It's stupid."

I informed him that things that never lived can't be stupid, but that made him madder. He poured the whole bottle of Magic Bubbles into my Granny's lily pond with the waxed crepe paper flowers. A few times Boomer's mother sent a game of Tiddly-winks, pick-up sticks, or jacks that Boomer and I might share. But, if I started to win, Boomer became fidgety and whipped out his Hopalong six-shooter.

"Bang, bang! You're dead."

I didn't like Boomer's toys as well as my special things in Uncle Judson's garage. My Uncle Judson shared all of his tools and drawing equipment with me. A concrete block building that did not yet have a fourth side or a complete roof, the garage was my happiest place to be. That's where I spent every afternoon between school and supper time consulting the big books of typefaces and lettering that stood on one shelf. Using the back side of my uncle's sign boards, I learned to plot out words, measuring the height and width of each letter to fit the space. Roman, Gothic, Helvetica Bold, Italic, Vogue. I loved the words. I lettered Boomer Merritt's name.

My favorite tool was a dark gray, cold metal vise mounted to the work bench. I liked to feel the sliding, turning rod; it held any object at any angle for me to study. What I longed for was a way to put events into the vice to hold them still, to figure them out. Uncle Judson might leave a dead bird or butterfly on his long work counter for me to copy. A drawing of a bird or a flower was special. Otherwise, people would frame the real things.

If my hands became tired, I had a special reading place on an old car seat propped against the wall beside seven years of Sears Roebuck catalogs. From those I learned the name of almost everything in the world. I did not invite Boomer to see my secret space. My mother never came in either. She said she might get grease on her good clothes because Uncle Judson was so sloppy.

One week, after they had fussed at me for not being friendly to Boomer, I carried blocks and lumber outside in the grass and built a ramp for his little steel cars. The top board was warped a bit, so that when Boomer positioned his car there, it rolled off the top board backwards and crashed in the grass. I showed him the depression in the board so he could help me turn it over, but instead he kicked the entire project apart. I was so glad his mother wanted him to live with her instead of us.

For Christmas, Mr. Merritt surprised my younger sister with a tricycle. To me he presented a shiny Hopalong Cassidy bicycle with training wheels and handlebars shaped like steer horns.

He pushed me forward on my bike to build up speed, and I was terrified. The ground moving under me was a blur. The crepe myrtles, with their magenta blossoms, became an unrecognizable streak of color.

"Look at Bonnie on her four-wheel bicycle, a Hopalong Ca-sissy," Boomer teased in a whining voice. He wanted to stage a holdup of some kids down the street, but I couldn't ride well enough to keep up with him. And I didn't know the plot.

That spring I received an Unsatisfactory in "Pays attention well." My mother took me to have my hearing tested, but nothing was wrong with my ears. No one asked me about the voice in my head who sang, recited verses to me, or scolded me at the same time the teacher might be giving instructions. I thought other kids must be able to hear everything I did but knew how to better pay attention.

"The best thing for a day dreamer," my teacher decided, "is to keep her busy." So I only went to class on Mondays for assignments and on Fridays for tests. In the office I decorated all the bulletin boards, cutting perfect Gothic letters out of construction paper. Then I was sent to the fourth grade to do a wall on dinosaurs and to the third grade to do "Children Around the World." That room had a globe with raised mountains. I saw that China was on the opposite side of the world from Atlanta, Georgia. Stone Mountain wasn't even there.

My project for the summer of 1952 was digging a hole to China. Because children were starving in China, my sister and I were always told to clean our plates by eating every bite. When I finished the hole, my sister was going to drop the vegetables she didn't like straight through to the Chinese children. In the early stages she helped me, but we got into a fight over how long each one of us should dig and she put a claw-forked garden tool into my elbow. I continued alone, progressing from spoons to a long stick to a shovel.

On July 4th, Boomer came for a picnic and produced a snake, which he promptly dropped down my hole. I could not risk killing the baby snake by poking it. I had a shoe box of roly poly bugs I had saved from the loose dirt that I could give to the snake, but I had to wait for the snake to crawl back out. If it came out at night, I might be postponing my project for no reason. Mr. Merritt said I was a cry baby.

On Labor Day, the Merritts came for another picnic. This time Boomer brought a length of white rope and a proposal. He wanted us both to swing so high at the same time that the front legs of the swing set would come out of the ground. Then we were to bail out and see if we could land on the other side of the rope, which he positioned in the grass like a finish line. On the count of three, we both started to swing as far back as we could.

Boomer told me to pull back on the chains and aim my feet straight up to the sky. I did what he said. The hooks on the supporting pole holding the chains of my swing seemed so close to my eyes that I could see them bending, preparing to break apart. I felt weightless and pressed my cheek hard against the chain. I closed my eyes. I couldn't hear what Boomer was saying.

Then he leaped, landing far out beyond the rope.

"Come on, sissy," he yelled at me. "It's your turn. Jump!"

Jump! My legs curled back under my seat. I tucked my head under my arm. Boomer called me an idiot. The swing began to slow down.

"You're so stupid," Boomer yelled at me. "You're just a dumb girl. The dumbest girl in the world!"

When my swing was low enough that I could reach the ground, I dragged my feet to slow it, and stopped the seat by grabbing it with my hand. Boomer came towards me with an ugly face and that cowboy swagger.

"You're no fun, you scaredy cat."

When he was close enough, I jumped out, holding still onto the metal seat, aiming it at his head. I'm usually not very good at hitting targets. I was surprised it hit him so hard. When Boomer was on the ground, I got the rope and tied his waist to the post of the swing. I used the square knot my Uncle Judson had taught me. Right over left. Then left over right. There. I went up the stairs, into the house, to my Granny's room.

I wish I *had* done that, but when my swing knocked Boomer down into the dirt, blood spilled from his head onto his lip and the fringes of his shirt turned brown. His mama came crying and shouting at me and took her son to the hospital. Then I went up the stairs, into the house, to my Granny's room.

That was the last time I ever saw Boomer Merritt.

For Halloween, Mr. Merritt brought my sister and me an orange plastic bank. When he put a nickel in, it lit up like a juke box and played a tune.

"Put another nickel in, in the nickelodeon. All I want is loving you and music, music, music," it sang.

He pulled us close to the buttons on his coat and promised to be good to us and my Granny, too.

Granny began to drop her spools of thread and scissors. One late afternoon she closed up the sewing machine, put up her hair, and opened the blinds.

"Go take a bath. Wash your neck good and your sister's, too."

"Are we going off, Granny?" I asked.

"Not me," she said.

Mr. Merritt came in a blue suit and drove us to a square brick house with a fluffy striped kitten on the steps. While the adults were inside, I sat on the steps with my sister and cradled the kitten. I found where her claws began to come out of her knuckles. When I covered her with my arm, she made a little cry.

A man in a black suit opened the screen door behind us and called me in. It was our Presbyterian minister, but I had never seen him away from the pulpit. My mother was sitting in a tall slip-covered chair. She had roses on the shoulder of her navy suit and a new gold ring on her hand. Tilting her head to one side, she smiled.

"Honey, come here. Mama is going to take a short trip with your new daddy. Then we will come back and get you and your sister. And go to a new house. I have to do this. Now you be a good girl. You and your sister will have your own room soon."

"What about Granny?" I wanted to know.

"We'll cross that bridge when we come to it," Mama said.

My sister and I went to bed. I could hear the adults talking in the kitchen. My aunt said she guessed it was "catch-as-catch-can" for my mother. Uncle Judson said he hoped "her chickens won't come home to roost."

Even though my mother went Christmas and birthday shopping for Boomer every year, Boomer never called on the telephone or wrote a Thank You letter. His dad took money every month to Boomer's mother, but one time Mr. Merritt was late, and she came to our front door with her flaming red hair and fur coat. She had a gun. Mama yelled for us to get under the beds. Once, I heard Mr. Merritt talk about saving money for Boomer to go to college.

"You better not," I heard Mama say.

Sometimes when I saw my stepfather looking at other people's sons, I knew he was wondering how big and tall Boomer might be. I had a fantasy that one day when Boomer was all grown up, he would come knocking at our door and ask to see me and say that he was sorry for calling me a dumbbell, because he really liked me all along.

You May Not Know It

You may not know it, but Joel Chandler Harris, who wrote down the stories told to him about the bear and the fox and the rabbit and the Briar Patch, gave me one of his wrens to hold.

My Granny held my hand as we walked to the corner of Gordon Street and Racine. Then she went back home to her sewing. If I turned to the right, I could see the giant pink house called the Wren's Nest where the Associate Editor of *The Atlanta Constitution* lived. As I got closer, I saw perched on the porch banisters big stuffed owls with round bulging eyes looking to see who was coming. I didn't see any birds' nests.

One time when it was cold, a wren made a nest in Mr. Harris' mailbox. And he didn't yell or shoo her away. He built another mailbox.

After he invited me to come in off the porch, Mr. Harris, who had thick red hair and freckles, opened the front windows with their long yellow curtains, followed by raising his arms and flying in a circle around the parlor. First, one little wren came hopping in and darted around the room, followed by two more. When he put the windows back down, the wrens perched on his shoulders and his head as he sat down to write. Then he turned around, called me, and laid a tiny brown bird from his desk in my hands. He told me the mother lays only one perfect egg each day. The tiny bird started to sing fast happy trills in its throat and looked up at me

Mr. Harris told me that his daddy disappeared like mine even before his parents had time to get married. He stammered when he talked so I guess that's why he memorized everything he read and wrote down stories out of the words.

I need to tell you something. Granny didn't walk me to the corner so I could see the Wren's Nest because my mother sold the house where I was born. It was really Aunt Willadeen and Uncle Judson's house that was near the Wren's Nest, but no one had time to take me to see it.

⌒

You may not know it, but I was an important collector of diamonds. I chiseled the sparkles from the grey rocks under the bushes on the way to Frank L. Stanton Elementary School. He was famous for writing the song "Keep a-Goin."

Most diamonds come from Africa, so it was a miracle that I spotted them in Atlanta. My Wonder Woman lunch box was so full of diamonds that I had to eat my bologna sandwich before recess to make room.

At home I stored the diamond chips under my bed in unused kitchen bowls. When I had ten pounds of diamonds, I took a yellow taxi downtown to a diamond and gold dealer on Forsyth Street that I found in the yellow pages. I sold them for a million dollars and gave all the money to the Atlanta public schools to hire Colored and White teachers who could tell good stories.

I continued to hide the new diamonds I gathered under my bed until spring cleaning when my mother, vacuuming under my bed, threw all my diamonds away and called them "Mere Malachite."

I need to tell you something. I wasn't a rich kid at all. I have my tiny savings account book with a red paper cover from when I was 13. The balance is $40.17. In my bedroom is a cream leather covered baby bank that my mother has been filling up with money since I was born. One day she will open it and give it to me.

~

You may not know it, but my father, the greatest artist in Georgia, painted so many beautiful poses of me that Mama must have given them all away to relatives. I never got to see my daddy painting because the President of the United States, Franklin Delano Roosevelt, invited him to come to Warm Springs to paint a big portrait of his dog Fala. While he was gone, my father called Mama every night, after I was asleep, to say how much he missed his precious little girl.

He also illustrated popular calendars for soldiers. At the end of the year, they probably threw them away. He worked for The Ruralist Press who printed all the yellow and white pages with telephone numbers for everybody and all the pictures of Coca Cola.

The other important thing you may not know is that I was the inspiration for the Morton Salt Girl on the round navy cardboard container. My mother told me.

You must have seen me. I was the brunette strolling confidently under my oversized, blue umbrella. I am holding a package of salt under my left arm, pouring it out behind me. I stroll forward; no one yells or scolds me for spilling. I am unafraid and happy. My image is on a shelf in every kitchen in America.

I need to tell you something. My father went to heaven when I was three years old. He never knew that I was always skinning my knees, so my Granny had to paint them bright orange with Mercurochrome, and that I walk with my head down to see better, afraid of stumbling on all the cracks in the sidewalk.

Childhood, Digital Collage from author's photos.
By Elizabeth Shepley, 2022.

Decomposed

My mother, who worked at Westview Cemetery, was the Executive Secretary to Asa Candler who owned the cemetery and the Coca Cola Bottling Company. Mama once took me to see the marble floors of the main building where she worked. On the walls hung almost a hundred stuffed and preserved heads of lions, tigers, wart hogs, panthers, and a thing with one horn, a rhinoceros, that had all died in Mr. Candler's private zoo. I stayed composed, like my teacher always said I was for my age, as their shiny, round black eyes followed me around the room.

My Granny and I walked to Westview Cemetery once a week after I got a cherry sucker with a string loop handle at a little market. On hot days, I would sip from the water fountain below the "For Whites Only" sign. The smaller, older fountain that was more my size had a sign above that read "For Colored Only," but if no one was looking, I would sneak a quick sip. She took me to the Uncle Remus library and to Woolworth's where I had a quarter to spend. My sister stayed home because she always let go of Granny's hand.

On a brass grave marker in the grass, under cherubs who spit water out of their round mouths, was my daddy's name, William Fred Henderson. Below his name, 1915-1947 marked the days he was born and died.

"Careful you don't step on a grave," Granny said. "You won't hurt them, but it's a matter of respect." I pictured the person's head resting under the marker, their legs and arms stretched down by their sides, asleep, and then I would walk around that shape.

One afternoon, Mama came home early with a red streaked face. A ground's keeper, who had watched her kneeling at my daddy's grave for two years, thought she had been grieving too long. Grabbing her arm, he pulled her over to a casket. He tore off the rug that covered it, pried off the lid, and forced her to look inside. I tried to get a full description of what she saw, but she said the body was decomposed and wasn't something for children to know about. She didn't look me or Granny in the eyes and there were long pauses between the short pieces of what she said, as if she were searching for words, but they had run away from her. I thought that dead people went back to God in heaven, but not in the same way they came. My Sunday school teacher said for certain that all babies came from God, but I didn't know how God got into a mother's stomach or why he would want us back after we finished living.

"What does 'decompose' mean?" I asked my teacher.

"Have you eaten all of your lunch?" she asked, not answering me.

At home I got a dictionary, went through all the words that started with "de" until I discovered that "decompose" meant "to break down into simpler parts."

I reasoned that a coffin might be like a supply box of the person's parts while he was on earth. Little piles of hair, teeth, rolls of skin, and bones all lined up by size like pencils. Or maybe when Mama looked in, everything was mixed up.

After the ground's keeper forced her to look at a decomposing body, Mama did not go back to Westview to work. Instead, she got a job working a switchboard with over 4,000 party lines at Southern Bell Telephone and Telegraph at 51 Ivy. She had to work on the top floor so all the wires could stretch out to other towns.

In December 1952, my big Christmas present that third grade year was a Toni doll. She came with a home permanent wave kit like the stinky one my mother used once to curl her hair. Toni's arms and legs, which were jointed to her chest and stomach, were hard wood, not soft rubber. She could sit, lean over, and stand. On her back was stamped **IDEAL DOLL P93.** Her eyes were gray under raised arched brows; she was curious about what was happening. She was the most beautiful doll in the world, and she never wanted to do anything mean. My Granny made Toni and me matching bridal veils with tiny ribbon forget-me-nots, matching aprons, and red plaid nightgowns.

Toni had dark glossy hair like mine, but the ends would curl instead of frizz. She came with pink roller curlers, small tissue papers to wrap sections of hair, and permanent wave setting solution that Mr. Merrit, my stepfather, said was only sugar water. One Saturday afternoon, the day Mama would roll up my hair and my sister's in brown rubber curlers so we would look pretty for church Sunday morning, I decided to roll Toni's entire head with curlers and setting lotion. I put her outside on the porch so she could see the stars while her hair dried. Sunday morning, her scalp was full of black ants, hundreds. When I tried to knock them away, clumps of Toni's hair fell in her lap.

For my big birthday present that year, I got another doll made by Madame Alexander. This doll had blonde hair, blue eyes, a pearl tiara, and a taffeta and net coral dress that was supposed to be like one that Queen Elizabeth had worn when she was young. I couldn't put homemade dresses on her and when I sat her in my lap to try to play with her, her long stiff arm poked me in the eye. All I could do with her was to hold her hand and walk her forward, causing her head to twist from side to side. I tried to walk forward while turning my head from side to side, but I couldn't do it at all. The Queen doll could only walk forward but not turn a corner or sit down. My Toni could do more than sit still to have her hair curled. Toni was alive.

I knew that the Queen Elizabeth doll must have cost a lot of money and that my mama wanted me to appreciate and love her for buying her.

"I did *not* take a second job to waste my money on you, young lady," Mama said, and I felt guilty for not loving the Queen doll.

On my birthday the week before Christmas, she placed a Spanky Patty doll with a bow on the back of its head at the foot of my bed. Spanky Patty was permanently crouched on her stomach with her thumb in her mouth and her behind sticking up. Her red pajamas would unbutton so she could be spanked, and except to make sure that her pajamas were always buttoned up, I never touched her. No matter what other dolls or stuffed animals I got for my birthday and Christmas, I only wanted my Toni doll. Once I had looked into her eyes, she became my most special friend.

Toni and I practiced dance and singing routines on our front porch. I tap danced in my recital costumes, and we did a Chinese dance with white powdered faces and parasols. I made a crepe paper parasol attached to a straw and secured it with a rubber band for Toni's right hand. Vance and Nancy from down the street started coming to our shows. Then I had a whooping idea. I could have Saturday morning talent shows and charge neighbor kids and their mothers a nickel.

I invited my sister to do a baton twirling number so she wouldn't pester me. I told the story of "Snow White and Rose Red," two sisters who are kind to a bear. I used hand motions, got on my knees to be the troll, stood on my tiptoes to growl like the bear. I tried to remember the words to all the Saturday morning television commercials like Captain Midnight's Hot Ovaltine song, Buster Brown's rhymes, "Sugar Pops are Tops," and "Use

Ajax, Boom, Boom," "Winky Dink and Me" and sang them as a duet with Toni. After seven months, we had a box full of coins.

My plan was to take the money Toni and I had made, and to leave on Thursday evening with Mr. Merrit's red flashlight. They would be at work on Friday and my Granny wouldn't say anything about my being gone. I didn't tell my sister anything or she would blab. On Thursday afternoon, I did my chores of dusting the baseboards in the living room and polishing the plant leaves. Then I hurriedly practiced the piano. When Toni and I left, I didn't want them to be mad at me for anything. My stomach felt like it was full of asparagus, green and ugly. I had to mash my shoulders back to keep my arms from coming off.

My Granny had made Toni and me matching traveling outfits with robin blue gabardine capes, pleated skirts, and pale-yellow blouses. In the attic, my mother had a three-piece Samsonite luggage set, but she never used the smallest one. In it I packed our suits and a change of underwear, our plaid jumpers, white blouses, and toothbrushes, but I didn't have room for our flannel nightgowns. Before dinner, I laid Toni on the bed next to the flashlight to rest up before our trip.

At supper, I pushed myself to eat everything on my plate, not to interrupt, and to take my plate and milk glass to the sink. The lights seemed too bright and the bickering too loud. All they said to me was, "Don't wash your food down your throat." When we finished eating, Mr. Merrit got up and stood in the doorway, his hands stretching up into the corners. I darted under his arm and went to my bedroom to put on my and Toni's going away suit.

Our suitcase was behind my bedroom door, but I couldn't find Toni. Where was Toni who had been napping on my bed? I looked everywhere, even under my bed. Finally, I had to go to the kitchen to ask through my tears if they had seen her.

"You can't find your doll?" my stepfather asked. "Maybe you better clean your glasses, kid," he laughed. "It's not like that damned doll could run away."

I went back to my bedroom and stood in the door, carefully scanning left to right. Up and down. Then I saw Toni's black shoes sticking up out of the waste can next to my twin bed. I ran to her and lifted her out. Her eyes wouldn't open when she was upright, so I shook her and shook her, but her right eye remained closed. When I twisted her leg down, it came off in my hand. The inside rubber band had busted, and all her parts were loose. Quickly I prayed for God to take life from one of my legs, cut it off, and give it to Toni who was 21 inches tall. I promised that if He could pull that off, Toni and I would tour A Live Doll Show all over the world. With all the money we would make, I would buy dolls and books and sewing machines for people who didn't have them. I could buy Mr. Merrit a brand-new trumpet like he had when he said he used to play at the Fox Theater downtown. I think he was happy then. I could buy my Granny bolts of rich silk fabric. Most of all, I wished I would make enough money to get my mother a live, real friend, so they could talk about what my mama really saw in the coffin that day that changed her eyes forever. Maybe by morning Toni would recover from being dropped on her head. I felt her forehead, and it was cold. It didn't matter. When the sun came up Friday, we would be long gone and far away.

The Empty Cross

I'm scared to do what Mary Sue and I are about to do. Mrs. Simmons, our day schoolteacher in summer, is marching all eight of us 4th graders to the Gordon Movie Theater. Mrs. Simmons leads from the front with her grey hair in a knot instead of those fluffy puffy hairdos women at my church wear, while I bring up the rear because I am responsible and can be trusted. Mary Sue walks in front of me and Melvin, tow-headed and part deaf, shuffles along in front of her. Across the street on our left is the Robert Hall Men's Store. Their sales song from the radio goes through my head:

Robert Hall this season/ Will show you the reason/ Low Overhead/Low Overhead

It's almost time for the 3 o'clock movie, *Creature from the Black Lagoon*, which will keep us occupied until our working parents can pick us up. One block before the Gordon Theater, we pass the Catholic Church on the right, bigger than my house, but smaller than a Baptist Church. The tall double doors always stand slightly ajar, and I glimpse hot sunlight streaking through the door and onto the cool marble floor. I am a baptized Methodist in the country and Presbyterian in the city, but Mary Sue is a Roman Catholic. My parents say that the Catholics pray to Rome and Jesus' mother, but not to God, and that they're the reason we have to eat fried fish sticks at school every Friday for lunch. Mary Sue says she has the right to go into any Catholic

Church in the whole world, but I can't, unless she sees fit to take me. And we must cover our heads.

She has agreed to take me today, so we break away from the line for the movies and sneak in. I take the two squares of fabric from my grandmother's quilt pieces and we place them over our hair. Although it is dark, we can see rows of pews, windows of colored shapes, and light coming from the front center as we proceed down the center aisle. I think this must be the altar like the Methodists have with two golden brass candlesticks on each side of a shiny cross. We walk slowly toward the light. There on the table burn many fat candles in jars, their wicks black and bent. Mary Sue says these hold prayers for the sick and dead.

On that table, as tall as my arm is long, is a cross that is not empty like those in my church but has Jesus hanging on it, with his head down, in terrible pain. What looks like barbed wire circles his head. His feet, fixed together with a square nail head, hang right ankle over left. There is a hole in his side, and I put my hand out to touch it when Mary Sue scolds me, "Don't touch. Or you'll drop dead."

Mary Sue gets down on her knees facing the altar and I copy her making the skirt of my dress spread all around, covering my lower half. After we keep our chins down like we are praying for two minutes, I look up and see a glorious, tall window with a pointed arch at the top. The navy sky is dark like a coming storm, but the summer sun shines through onto the figure of Jesus in colored glass.

His face is streaked with dirt and blood, and he is crying. His robe is ripped. Blood pours down from the wound in his right side and dried blood is caked around the holes in his feet and hands. His arms, spread wide, are bound by ropes to the cross bar, and each palm is pierced with a black nail. I've never seen such hurt in a picture before or a person being treated so cruelly except for the postcard I have at home of a lynched man hanging from a tree with a rope around his neck, his body sagging and dead.

I wander down the aisle, past the sides of the pews, looking over my shoulder every few steps, to see if Jesus is still crying. Why was he being punished after he told so many good stories and fed five thousand people? My blessing at home before we can eat says, "God is great, God is good. Let us thank Him for our food." If He were really great, He would have stopped mean people from killing his own son. And if He were good, He would have told his son to get out of town, wouldn't He? On the sides of the pews, under the pink and gold decorations on the ceiling, there are four statues of angels standing next to four men who Mary Sue says wrote the first five books in the Bible. She stands behind the tallest and flaps her arms, so we start playing hide and seek between the marble figures, putting our arms around their legs.

I startle when the door behind us creaks and Mrs. Simmons' voice says searchingly, with worry, "Are you girls in here?" I think of lying flat on the floor under the pews to hide but Mary Sue answers, "Yes, Ma'am. We got hot outside."

"Get yourselves to this door immediately," she scolds. "There will be hell to pay for this." Before we go back out onto the hot sidewalk, she strikes our backsides three times each with the flat of her hand and squeezes our wrists, yanking us out the heavy doors where all the other kids are waiting. We are made to stand in line directly behind her now.

Mrs. Simmons says nothing more to us, but when our parents come to pick us up, she hands them each a Mason jar with her Prescription for Good Children, light brown and made from

Milk of Magnesia, Syrup of Pepsin, and a dash of Castor Oil. If Mrs. Simmons had told on me and Mary Sue, we would have been switched all over our legs and arms, but she didn't tell on us. I figured that she didn't want our parents to know she hadn't kept track of us during the seventy-five-cent movie.

At home I can't ask Mama about what I had seen or why the Methodists and Presbyterians hid Jesus' suffering, bleeding, and dying from us. Maybe it would keep people from wanting to be near the gold cross. My stepdaddy would have yelled and hit me and made me stay inside on the weekend if he knew what I had done.

When my relatives passed to the hereafter, Mama would bring the wire stands and green-wrapped wreaths from the cemetery home to keep because she didn't want the wind to knock them over or for anyone to steal them to use on a stranger's plot. The big green foam crosses on wire easels were covered in white flowers, sometimes lilies and carnations. The crosses were beautiful, not at all like those Catholic crosses, but after three days the flowers would begin to wilt, their heads would fall, they would turn brown, and die in our hallway. Then Mama would strip the crosses and wreaths and store them in the bottom of the hall closet across from our bathroom.

In the fall after my Granny came to look after me because Mrs. Simmons said I was too big and smart for her other children, I started hiding unseen on the third shelf in that closet. When Granny took her late afternoon nap. I would first place one of the crosses on the shelf above. Then I would climb up by placing my knee on the shelf, drawing my head and shoulders in, before finally pulling up my other leg. Up there, I would try to mash my body flat on top of the cross to see what it felt like. I thought about what I had seen in the window of the Catholic

Church: Jesus in tears and dried blood, ugly knotted muscles, pale skin with the blood draining out, but somehow beautiful. At first, what remained of the dried-up flowers sounded like breaking Ritz crackers, and the wire frame would poke me. My arms were longer than the cross piece, so I would tuck my hands under, digging my fingers into my palms. When I tried to stretch out, my ribs seemed to come apart. Hanging heavy from nails, Jesus' ribs must have separated, too. I couldn't raise my head under the shelf above, so I lay as still as possible until I conformed to the rough, rugged cross, and could no longer feel it beneath me at all. I felt alone. But on my small cross, I was hidden and safe, until I had to get down and drop my feet to the floor.

Honor

My parents decided my sister and I were too big to go to nursery school, and all our schedules were too hectic since Mama had transferred from downtown to a suburban U. S. Army satellite office of records. The new elementary school, Arkwright, was almost complete but without grass, trees, or a flagpole. Mama said Arkwright would be a better school than People Street Elementary because the principal was the brother of my Presbyterian pediatrician. Since it was only four streets away from our home, we would have a chance to meet kids in our neighborhood, and I could be in class with the girls from my Presbyterian church.

Anytime Miss Womack opened her middle desk drawer and took out the boxes of colored stars, my sixth-grade class became quiet. We had already had two teachers quit who didn't award stars. Now the B papers got red stars, most of the A's received blue stars, but if there were exceptional papers, Miss Womack handed out large silver ones. Those who made C's or D's received nothing and picked up their work in silence after class.

"Remember, class, what we decided," said Miss Womack. "Those who earned the highest marks on these papers would be our cloakroom judges for the month of April. I have a special black folder in which I want them to list all the charges and punishments they decree." I was one of the four girls on the front row who had waited with anticipation for Miss Womack to make her announcement. "The best essays on honor and justice were written by Valerie Matthews, Jenny Allen, Mary Lou Norris, and Bonnie Henderson."

I knew Miss Womack would like my paper because I had quoted Shakespeare's *King Henry IV*, in which Sir John Falstaff speaks about honor:

"What is honor? A word. What is that word, Honor? Air. A grim reckoning!"

I argued that only justice could be measured, for honor was something we bestowed on others when they performed acts of which we either are not capable or do not wish to undertake like Brutus eliminating Caesar, sacrificing the countless dead in the Civil War to assuage guilt over slavery, Presidents and Senators on whom we could blame the state of the nation. So, I had decided not to call the meeting place of the judges an Honor Court. I had already made a sign in careful lettering that read "Cloakroom of Justice."

I had also written a list of probable offenses with the appropriate punishment and had shown them to my friends.

"Miss Womack," Jenny shouted, "Bonnie has already made out a list of offenses." Miss Womack fluffed her full black skirt and perched herself on the edge of her desk.

"Read the laws, Bonnie," she prompted me. "Class, listen for the principles of fairness we have been discussing."

I bit off the eraser of my Coca-Cola pencil, swallowed it quickly, and began to read. "One. If a student talks when Miss Womack is out of the room, he will have to be quiet all during recess.

"Two. If a student sharpens his pencil while Miss Womack is talking, he will have to stay in after school and sharpen all the pencils in the teacher's desk.

"Three. If a student asks his neighbor what he made on a test or brags about a mark, he will be given unmarked papers for two weeks.

"Four. If a student keeps a messy desk, he will have to stay after school and help the janitor for half an hour.

"Five. If a student steals bus money or sandwiches or cookies from lunch boxes; if a student is caught gossiping or spreading rumors, he will confess to the victim and write a note to his parents.

"Six. If a student copies from an encyclopedia, he will have to find five other books on the subject and turn the list in to Miss Womack.

"Seven. If a student signs his parents' name to his report card, his parents will be notified that all his papers must be signed every day for a month.

"Eight. A group of five students may request that any one in class be judged for an infraction that disrupts teaching, but the reporting students must be present at the trial.

"Nine. A punishment may be lessened if a student comes to the Cloakroom of Justice with a witness to explain unseen reasons for the offense.

"And ten. All decisions of the judges are final, as of this date, April 9, 1956." Making a note that I had read the rules to the class, I chewed on my pencil again, forgetting that the eraser was gone, and cut a small slice out of my lip with the metal end.

Miss Womack made the announcement and gave us an assignment.

"The Judges will meet every Friday in the cloakroom during recess. Now, I'm going to take your lunch money to the cafeteria. Start answering the ten questions at the end of the social studies chapter that you read for homework."

We all groaned, a ritual, because we always had to answer the questions at the end of the chapter. I had found that it was not efficient to read a chapter before answering the questions; it made more sense to read the questions and then look for the answers.

On tests, Miss Womack always picked information from picture captions to trick us.

The only way to make an "A" in sixth grade was to make impressive, well-done Product Maps, which Miss Womack was crazy for. Product Maps were large sheets of poster paper with a map of Brazil, Australia, or China in the center. Radiating spokes led to the edges where the products were displayed. While my classmates drew pictures of the products or cut them out of magazines, my forte was using actual samples, which sometimes had to be encased in clear plastic, especially flour, coffee, and corn meal. The only thing that worried me about these maps was that I had cut a square of silk out of my mother's best dress for China's silk. She had not yet discovered it, and there was a chance she might never have an occasion to take the jade green dress out of the special bag in her closet. Later I was sorry I had cut the dress, but at the time I didn't think about my mother, only about my Product Map.

Once Miss Womack was out of the room, Randy, the slow-thinking red headed boy on the back row, punched the taller boy, Jerry, in front of him.

"Hey, Jerry, my pencil is under your desk," Randy's easily distressed whisper projected down the aisle. "It's got my name on it."

"Who cares?" Jerry replied, stretching his long penny loafer under his desk to flip the pencil into the aisle where it rolled over three rows and finally stopped in front of the radiator.

"Look where you kicked my pencil!" Randy wailed. "I can't reach it without getting out of my seat."

Jerry ignored him and proceeded to move his finger under each word of the questions, mouthing the words separately.

"Please get my pencil, Jerry," Randy begged.

Instead, Jerry clapped his hand over his mouth, made a muffled noise, and pointed at Randy as I turned and gave them both a disapproving look.

"The Judges are watching you," Robert Register, in his thick glasses, whispered to Jerry.

"You get to go to the cloakroom," Nancy Henson giggled and chided, jingling her charm bracelets.

"All right," Judge Jenny snapped. She jumped up, snatched a piece of notebook paper and marched to the back of the room. "Who all is talking back here?"

"Jerry knocked my pencil over there and I can't do my questions."

"Get Randy's pencil," Jenny commanded Jerry who sauntered up in his tight jeans, flipped his duck tail back and recited so all the class could hear:

"Order in the court,
Judges gotta spit.
Who can't swim,
Better git."

Bursts of laughter broke from the class.

"Order in the court!" Randy chanted, banging on his desk. "Order in the court!"

With an admiring gaze, near-sighted Robert watched as Jerry retrieved the pencil, sucked it into his mouth, and then blew it like a rocket ship across three rows of desks to land in front of Randy.

The class only began to work on the questions in earnest when they heard Miss Womack talking outside the door. Soon she came in, patting her black skirt.

"The principal thinks that having judges will be a good experience for the class," she told us. "So, before recess, if the judges have any names, they should list them on the board."

I gave my list to Valerie, and she wrote on the board: *Randy O'Daniell, Nancy Henson, Robert Register, Jerry Jones*.

The cloakroom was a light blue, narrow, long room with pull-up doors, a rack for coats and lunch boxes, and four chairs for the judges. Jenny read the charges and Mary Lou wrote down all comments.

"Randy O'Daniell started talking as soon as Miss Womack left the room," read Jenny.

"I didn't either," said Randy. "Jerry knocked my pencil under the radiator, and he wouldn't go get it."

"Did you ask him nicely?" I queried.

"Yeah, and that's when I broke your dumb rule," he mumbled.

"You should come to school prepared with more than one pencil," Valerie told him. "Your punishment will be listed on the board."

"Who's next?" we asked.

"Nancy Henson."

"I bet she has seventy-five charms – and they're real gold too."

"Have you seen her angora sweater? My mother said I couldn't have one until I stopped growing."

"I bet she puts powder on her skin, don't you think?"

"She was definitely talking, so we have to keep her in. Let's just tell her."

"Yeah."

"Next."

Robert Register came in slowly twisting his head to look at the coat racks and the light bulb over his head.

"Sit down, Robert," we ordered.

"Robert Register was talking when Miss Womack was out of the room and he was making fun of the Judges," read Jenny.

Robert took off his glasses, pulled a handkerchief out of his pocket, blew on the glass, and rubbed a smear of ink that had dried in the crescent of his bifocals. "I just whispered," he said, squinting his pale blue eyes.

"Who heard him?" I asked.

"I did," said Valerie.

"So did I," said Jenny.

"I was only whispering," Robert insisted. We sent him out.

"Let's not let him play ball with the other boys."

"What good will it do? He never plays anyway because he can't judge how far away the ball is."

"I can't play ball and I don't like recess," I said.

"We can't make any exceptions," they said. "The penalty for talking when the teacher is out of the room is staying in for recess."

"Okay," I said, "but it's a briar patch to Robert."

"Why don't we just tell Jerry Jones the same thing?" Jenny asked before adding, "I have to go to see the nurse. I might have started my period, you know."

I didn't personally know anyone who had started yet, but before I could ask Jenny for details and symptoms, the cloak-room door flew up and in strolled Jerry Jones, almost as tall as the light bulb, with half a sandwich in one hand and an apple in his mouth.

"We're not supposed to eat until lunch time, Jerry." Valerie chastised "And, you're not allowed to eat in the class either,"

Jerry grunted. "I'm hungry now," he stated. Pulling the apple from his teeth, he offered us a bite.

"Read the charges," I said, trying not to look at him. He was really cute, and he was taller than me.

"I was talking when Miss Womack was out of the room." Jerry recited in a sing-song cocky tone.

"What about Randy's pencil?"

"He's always losing them. That's why his mama has his name put on them," Jerry told us, smiling. "Is there a law you can't help someone get their pencil? It's not my fault that the damn thing rolled under the radiator. Is there a law?"

"We'll have to talk about your case privately," we told him although I admired his adult-sounding defense.

"Why don't you let me stay for your meeting?" He winked at me. "It might do me some good, you know, to associate with the four smartest girls in class." He smiled at us. He had beautiful teeth and no braces.

"You're not supposed to," I said to him. "We won't need you to help us reach our decision."

"Well, I think maybe I'll stay in the cloakroom and kiss the judges," he said smiling.

Mary Lou and Jenny quickly stepped outside the pullup door. Valerie giggled and hid her face. I stood still, frozen. I could hear the class running in the hall, and Miss Womack raising her voice to them. Jerry grabbed me and hugged me so tight I couldn't breathe. He put his whole mouth on mine and pushed my lips open. The piece of peanut butter and jelly sandwich he passed me was the sweetest thing I'd ever tasted. All the words in my head vanished as if wiped off by a brand-new eraser.

"Time's up, girls," Miss Womack called as she approached the cloakroom. "Let's have the verdicts. Jerry, get to your seat."

Jenny, Mary Lou, Jerry, and Valerie went to their seats, and I took the record book from Jenny. I marked in it the decisions. Then I went to the board and numbered one to four. I erased number four and printed with my decisive lettering:

The Cloakroom of Justice Committee-Miss Womack's Sixth Grade Randy O'Daniell can't talk during recess tomorrow.

Nancy Henson can't talk during recess tomorrow.

Robert Register can't talk during recess tomorrow.

My face felt sunburned and my heart fluttered as I walked unsteadily back to my seat.

Jerry was not a good student, but he had a kind of knowl-edge about things and a magic energy that my smart girlfriends didn't have. For the rest of the school year, I don't think I barely said one word to Jerry Jones, but I watched him when he wasn't looking at me.

The Age of
Accountability

In December of 1956 I turned 12, the Age of Accountability. That meant that God would *now* start keeping track of my sins. That meant that the year *before*, when I cut a piece of Mama's best navy silk dress for a map of China showing important products, it didn't count. Bad things like that one I had done by myself, alone.

Yet, sometimes bad things happened that people didn't do, like in the sixth grade when all the girls got head lice. Most girls' heads got shaved and they wore scarves to school. Mama wouldn't cut my hair off, so I had to be bathed with stinking, stinging tar soap and shampoo. Are insects accountable?

There were also bad things I could be part of without actually doing anything except going along with the deed, like when my whole class knew that Randy and Allen, who had to be watched for bad behavior, let the milk in the rubber nipple stay up too long. The milk spilled down onto the floor before mean, old Miss Milam could come down the counter with her beige plastic tray and stop it. I imagined her slipping on the wet tile, breaking her hip, and dying. I could hear her screaming when we ran.

Yet, when Miss Milam's right foot skidded backwards in the milk, and she grabbed the counter, the boys stepped back. We girls looked horrified and gasped, "Oh, no." The lunchroom grew

as quiet as dawn, but none of us called or went for help. As punishment, we had a boring teacher the rest of the year; she didn't
know how to tell stories.

That summer, Mama had Granny sleep in the den during the
week so that someone would be home with me and my sister.
There was not much to do for the summer except sew with
Granny, draw lots of trees with bird's nests, and check out books
for the reading program at the library. The City of Atlanta had
closed the swimming pools and park recreation programs due
to impending integration. Only White children could check out
books in the library. Because Mama called every afternoon to see
what we were doing, I always answered the phone immediately
so she would not worry, but this time all I heard was breathing
and whispers. I thought something was wrong with the phone.

"Can you hear me?" I asked.

"I like your voice," a man said. "You're the girl with the red
sweater who walks up the street to school aren't you? So pretty."

Suddenly, I realized that a stranger had been watching me.

"Sometimes," I replied slowly. "Who are you? Are you a friend
of my parents? Maybe I shouldn't be talking to you."

"I won't hurt you. I'll only make you feel good. Are you by
yourself?"

"No, my Granny is here, and my mama is coming home in a
few minutes."

"That's okay. I just need you to talk to me for a little while. Say
'Oh my, that is so big.' Say it again. And again. Say 'I want to hold
you in my hand so bad, so much. Say that again.'"

The man made a sound in the back of his throat like a kitty
coughing up a hair ball. I thought maybe he was sick at his

stomach, but then he started breathing loudly, faster, and faster, until he suddenly stopped.

"Talk to me some more, pretty girl. Whisper. Say you want to see me."

"I don't. And I am going to hang up."

"Go ahead. Do that. I know where you live."

My hand was shaking when I put the receiver down. Because that man said he knew where I lived, I told Mama when she got home. Since he saw me go to school, he must live on my street. Mama told me not to be scared, that she would report the call and someone would take care of him.

A few days later, Mama did not go to work. She said we had to go to a special office at Fort Mac that was investigating the phone call to me. She said it was a serious crime.

"But he didn't really hurt me," I told them.

"Why didn't you hang up when you knew it wasn't your mother?" the officer asked.

In the special office I sat at a grey metal table. Before me was a glass wall with four men behind it in separate chairs with their heads down. One was bald and scratching his ear. The Army officer in charge said he wanted me to listen carefully to each man until I heard the same voice as the one who had talked to me on the phone. Each man was made to say "I won't hurt you, but I know where you live. I've seen you, pretty girl."

One by one they raised their heads to repeat the words. One of them was big with muscles in his arms, his sleeves rolled up to show a tattoo of a rose. Another one looked straight into my eyes as if he knew me somehow. I couldn't help but stare back.

"Well, what do you think?" the officer asked.

"They're talking too loud. Get them to whisper."

So they whispered, but I couldn't imagine a full body attached to the voice that had talked to me.

"Don't look at them. Just listen," ordered the officer. I put my head down and only listened, but I could still remember each one. "Which one is it?"

"None," I said.

"Are you sure?" he asked, and I nodded. "Let's do this again. Whisper your lines."

Again I tried to listen, but they were too far away, not close to my ear. "I don't know. I can't pick."

"I want you to point at the one who sounds most like the man who called you."

The man with sandy hair, the youngest, was still staring at me, but he seemed like a kind person. The man with the tattoo seemed too strong and gruff. The other two were vacant bodies.

"None of them are the right one."

"Listen, honey," Mama said, coming over to sit beside me, "one of these men, an Army Sergeant, lives at the top of our street and he has been in jail once for calling a little girl and scaring her to death. They had to let him out because the girl wouldn't come into the court room."

"Maybe he wasn't the right man," I said.

"But you can pick him now," she said, "and then he can't ever hurt anyone else." I said I couldn't. She said I had to.

The Army officer in charge then stood behind the youngest man and asked me if I was certain it was not him. I was not certain. He made the man whisper "*I have seen you, pretty girl,*" looking intensely at me.

"Maybe it is that man," I said.

"Thank you," the officer said and patted my shoulder. Mama said we could go home.

The six-room GI houses on our street had only three designs; that man's house was exactly like ours, white with a big front porch from which he must have watched me. He had two

66

daughters like Mama did. In a few weeks I saw the orange Ajax moving truck come and a For Sale sign sprout up in the red dirt and sparse grass. Whether he was the right man or the wrong man, my words had ruined his family's life. I wished I could bite off my tongue.

Our teacher in sixth grade, Mrs. Langley, was wonderful. For kids who got bored, she had all sorts of posters and information in big print around the room to read. A book rack of orange bound biographies was available for us to take home. She told us stories about Amelia Earnhardt, Joan of Arc, Clara Barton, George Washington Carver, and Albert Schweitzer. She never talked about the Civil War. She had a bob of dark hair and sparkling eyes.

In September, she wore high heels. By Christmas, she had switched to lace up flat shoes and started getting chubby and patting her stomach, leaning back against the blackboard. In January, the principal came in to tell us we would have a new teacher for the New Year. Mama told me Mrs. Langley couldn't teach because she gotten herself pregnant. Our next teacher only gave out faded purple papers with questions on them to which even she didn't know the answers.

Three afternoons a week I walked from school to a ballet and tap dance studio where I made $1.25 an hour to demonstrate steps for second graders. On Thursdays I went to piano lessons at Miss Gloria Griffin's. A picture on her living room wall showed Miss Griffin sitting at the piano on her hip length brown hair. She had been beautiful but had never married. Her home was lovely and filled with mahogany furniture. My mother said her father must have left her some money because a woman alone could never support herself and have nice things.

On the way to piano that year, I cut through a back yard at the top of my street one day and literally ran into a ninth-grade boy named Jimmy Gordon. My music books were strewn all over the ground and he picked them up for me. I was twelve and he was fourteen, as tall as I was, and the first boy I knew who shaved. He had, in fact, a small mustache across his sensuous upper lip, deep brown eyes with long lashes, and wavy hair. Sometimes when I saw him, he was not wearing a shirt. I saw him every Thursday. I told my sister, who promptly told my mother, that my piano teacher wanted me to come early so I could get used to the touch on her new grand piano. Was it a lie if it didn't come from me?

Jimmy Gordon had a battery radio and he played Elvis Presley's "That's All Right, Mama." He said he liked Elvis but that his parents thought Elvis was vulgar. I liked that word. *Vulgar.* Everyone knew, so we were told, that boys who scratched you in the palm of the hand or told banana and basket jokes were vulgar, too. That Colored women who sat with their legs spread on steps of old apartment buildings smiling at the passersby were vulgar. That women who smoked in public or talked too loud on the sidewalk were also vulgar, my mother said.

Jimmy didn't act vulgar. He brought me daisies. Because his father was an Army Colonel stationed at Third Army, Fort McPherson, Jimmy could tell me stories about England, France, and Germany, and how the tiny Japanese girls with their small waists and feet dressed peculiar. Right away I started doing fifty side to side bending exercises every morning. He said my eyes listened. I started brushing my eyebrows with my toothbrush. He said he would like to see me dance, so one day I wore my leotards under a raincoat and danced for him around a tree.

"Wowie, zowie," he responded.

Jimmy had a record of Elvis singing "Long Tall Sally" that he wanted me to dance to. I said my mother wouldn't allow me to go in his house to hear it, so he put his record player on full volume and opened his window. Out on the lawn of his house, he taught me to fast dance, and then he asked me to go to a party at Fort McPherson. His parents would drive.

When I asked my mother about it, I was certain she would say no, but she didn't. She didn't even ask me if I wanted to go, but she bought me a dress that was strapless with uncomfortable stays to keep the top from sliding down. I was afraid to twist or raise my arms. Below I wore a garter belt to hold up sheer stockings. She made an appointment for me to have my hair done and told me to polish my fingernails.

Soon all the relatives and my mother's friends were teasing me about Jimmy, acting as if I had finally made a choice to like boys instead of books. They all seemed happy as if a long sought-after goal had been reached.

Jimmy and his parents came to pick me up in a big brown Army limousine. He wore a white sport coat and brought me a corsage of pink carnations. My mother tried to photograph his pinning the corsage to my dress, but I screamed at her and fled to the bathroom to fasten the flowers on my strapless bodice myself. The elbow length white gloves made everything feel unreal. And special.

The Officer's Club was decorated with crepe paper streamers and over-sized bright flowers. A kaleidoscope projector sent shimmers of multi-colored lights into every corner of the room, making me dizzy. Everyone was dashing about saying hello and kissing each other on the cheek. I stumbled over several chairs before deciding to wear my glasses.

The women seemed to glide on the arms of their escorts. They drank a lot and brought me a pretty drink called a Shirley Temple. I quickly learned to dance with a partner. Mostly after I learned where to put my arms, I just stepped to the right and then to the left. With his hand on my back, Jimmy tried to pull me closer and closer until a man in uniform tapped Jimmy on the shoulder and I had to dance with him.

"You sure are a pretty girl," he whispered, smashing me against his chest and thighs.

Jimmy's father and some other men asked me to dance slow dances. "May I have the honor of this dance, Miss?" They didn't expect any answer but, "Of course" or "I'd love to."

Their big chests, decorated with bars, ribbons, and medals, seemed like plated armor. I felt crushable.

By the time the women were sitting in a stupor at their tables, I was bone tired. My date and the other teenagers had gathered outside to look at the insides of a car. The officers gathered at the bar to toast General Eisenhower who had been re-elected President. Two had had the distinct honor of serving under him. "So had some nurse!" they roared, laughing. They mimicked the Japanese, pulling their eyes out to thin slits like little boys will do. They made fun of the Germans, the French, the English, and the Hawaiians. They told gory stories and made grand gestures. They described new weapons that would leave nothing behind for a medic to repair.

They said Eisenhower integrated the Army to keep the Colored battalions from killing each other and mimed those same soldiers trying to read training manuals. Then they started in on "pieces of ass,"–Colored ones, yellow ones, shaved ones, old ones, fresh ones.

"And if you tell a dame she's beautiful, she'll do anything you say and forgive you afterwards," they told one another.

I was stunned. What was I supposed to do if other people, especially adults, were ugly and prejudiced? I couldn't be held accountable for them, could I?

In the car going home, Jimmy whispered into my ear asking if I would meet him before school in his backyard. I didn't answer yes or no. If you kissed boys, you might get pregnant, lose your job, and have to be poor or get married. Didn't everyone know that?

Under the light of my porch, I did whatever was necessary to say "Thank-you-for-a- lovely-evening" and rushed inside where my mother and stepfather were both waiting to hear about my first date. Again, I said whatever was necessary to please them and went to bed. From smiling, standing straight, smiling, dancing, smiling, having to hold my body distanced, smiling, listening, and smiling some more, my body hurt all over.

In a few days Jimmy called me to tell me that I was the most beautiful girl at the dance and that I should cut my piano lesson to come over and hear "Party Doll" in his house.

"I want to take you to another dance," he said, adding, "I might even buy you an orchid."

"That sounds nice," I said, "but my stepfather says I can't date for a few more years. He's very strict. And very mean."

Justice

"Why that isn't big enough to hold the tear drops of a dirt dauber," my stepfather's mother said, eying my first bra.

In the bathroom, I had taken a measuring tape and measured my rib cage. Then I leaned forward at the waist so that my rosy nipples and fat deposits fell forward. In this position I had determined that I needed a B cup, but my mother, who had not seen me naked since I was a baby, had bought me a size AAA, which was on sale at Rich's Department Store where she worked on weekends and holidays.

When the Russians sent up Sputnik I and II, state governors and Boards of Education started talking about how we should have more science but our teachers hadn't had any science, either. Although there was a poster in our seventh-grade class of the phases of the moon, I only knew that the Man in the Moon was being punished for working on the Sabbath. No one seemed curious about outer space or if there were other universes and worlds with other creators. People seemed only emulous of the Russians doing something the U.S. had not done first.

I made a current events bulletin board for my class with articles about Adlai Stevenson and his ideas for international bans on testing H-bombs. I was awed by the prospect of thousands of tons of earth, buildings, rocks, glass, arms, and legs being pulverized and thrown high into the air. In the event of a hydrogen bomb attack, we were to go into the basement of a school or crouch near an inside wall. Our new school had neither, so once a week we marched outside to lay face down in the dirt. Above all, we were cautioned not to look at the blast, yet I knew with certainty that I would look.

On the third anniversary of Brown vs. the Board of Education, a Baptist preacher from Atlanta, Martin Luther King, Jr., led a march for voting rights in May in front of the Lincoln Memorial. I liked Ike because under him it became the law that everyone except Indians could vote and go to school.

"Integration in schools should start with the upper grades of high school," some experts said. "At that age, they'll behave in a mature way."

"Integration should start in first grade," another group of experts argued. "At that age, they won't know any better." Clearing their throats, they corrected, "Know any difference."

One day our teacher, rumored to be in favor of a teacher's union, grew so frustrated with our class that she said she "would rather teach Negroes" than us. Some kids told their parents, so the principal called her to his office, where my stepfather said she refused to apologize.

That fall, President Eisenhower sent a thousand U.S. troopers into Little Rock, Arkansas, to ensure the safety of nine students attempting to integrate the high school. Clustered in the fellowship hall after church, the adults angrily argued.

"The federal government has no right to interfere in the policies of our state," they proclaimed.

"Yankees always overdo everything," they complained. "Especially if it gives them the opportunity to cram it down the Southerner's throat!" And on they went, spitting angry words.

My parents said that as long as the schools were integrated, my sister and I would never go to school with Colored children, so they put us on a waiting list to be interviewed for enrollment in Westminster Schools, started by Atlanta leaders in 1951. My stepfather wouldn't have much time to drive us across town and then get himself and Mama to work. Later, I heard them talk about mortgaging our house for the tuition at the private Christian school.

Over the holidays, our teacher suffered a nervous breakdown and quit. Our new teacher, Mrs. Wilson, was pregnant. Parents were upset that a teacher could be in the classroom after she was showing, but since there was a substantial shortage of new and substitute teachers, and the older teachers were electing early retirement before integration came, nothing much could be done about it. The state and federal governments had offered loans and scholarships to help persuade men and women to major in education, so Mrs. Wilson was the only person available to take our class for the remainder of the year. I worried that her baby might be born during an atomic attack, that she would be killed, and I would have to care for it not knowing what to do.

Dreamy eyed, but a solid, tall woman, Mrs. Wilson was not easily ruffled. From the beginning, she let us know that she was doing us a favor by being our teacher.

"I will accept no nonsense," she told us. "I intend to read every word of your American history papers," As most of the class groaned, she added, "and I can recognize sentences from any encyclopedia in print."

I already had twenty pages written on my project, planning to add one page on each battle of the Civil War and hand drawn illustrations of all the uniforms.

Soon after she arrived, Mrs. Wilson changed my atomic power bulletin board to the subject of civil rights. She put up articles on the new Southern Christian Leadership Conference and in big letters printed the words of Abraham Lincoln: "Those who deny freedom to others, deserve it not for themselves." She also put up a photograph of that Baptist preacher from Atlanta and his wife at a midnight ceremony celebrating the independence of Ghana, which put me to thinking about people worldwide not being free to live like everyone else could. Mrs. Wilson's baby had begun to kick, and I thought I could see her dress jump across her stomach.

Mrs. Wilson said we were not being challenged by our textbooks.

"True education is sometimes found in the community rather than in books," she told us. "And as long as you can behave, we will plan for spring field trips."

Our first trip was to Crawford W. Long Hospital for White people where I had been to have my tonsils out. Colored people had to go to Grady Hospital where the back two wards were for them. We saw an exhibit about Crawford W. Long, the physician who had removed a tumor from James Venable's neck while the patient slept at home in Jefferson, GA. The vapors of ether would put men to sleep so they could have their limbs sawed off or bullets dug from out of their stomachs and chests in relative comfort. Well-to-do soldiers in the Civil War had only morphine laudanum, and opium gum to ease pain, but not to put them to sleep.

At a small museum at Emory University, we saw a replica of the black basalt Rosetta Stone, duplicating in three languages the reign of Ptolemy III. The museum had Egyptian mummies and a young boy's sarcophagus decorated to look like the body of a prince, but an x-ray disclosed that the corpse inside was the bottom section of an adult's leg—the kneecap resembling a head and the calf a torso. I started to wonder if other parts of history might be a trick, not by historians, but by the people being studied. We saw replicas of the Great Pyramids and the Sphinx, and I learned that the people responsible for these wonders of the world were dark skinned.

Our next class trip was to a rehearsal of the Atlanta Symphony Orchestra. I was in our Presbyterian church choir, I had played the triangle at Frank L. Stanton Elementary, and I had played one piece on the clarinet in the Arkwright Junior Band. We always sounded like separate people practicing because we were so worried about getting our parts right that we couldn't look at the conductor. I had never been exposed to any group enterprise in which everyone knew his part and the design of the whole piece so well that the sound and harmony of the whole became a great and splendid thing.

On May 1, our history projects were due, and I wanted mine to be the best in the class. I finished my report's cover sketch of Robert E. Lee just before I had to catch the bus. When I turned in my thick, beautiful project, Mrs. Wilson said, without even looking inside, that she couldn't grade it because she didn't have time to read it.

"I'm paid to be fair and to give the same amount of time to each student," she said. "I am afraid you have misunderstood the purpose of the assignment to become familiar with the library and to follow the report format."

The traditional spring trip by bus to Washington, D.C. was the biggest event in the seventh grade. For certain, all members of the Safety Patrol, the A students, would go. We wore a silver badge, a shoulder strap, and a belt of white webbing. An hour before and after school we were assigned to street corners to help the younger children cross. Since I could not judge distance or speed, if I saw a car at all, I wouldn't let my charges cross.

But then Mrs. Wilson changed the rules and insisted that everyone in the seventh grade make the trip, even the people who could not read well. She collected money from the school board and her friends for students who could not afford the bus fare.

"Either everyone goes," she said, "or no one goes."

So on May 15, our class boarded the bus to ride all night to our nation's capital.

On the streets of Washington, D.C. I saw my first Colored men dressed in suits and ties and carrying briefcases. Back home, I had only seen people's maids on the bus wearing faded clothes and run-down-at-the-heel slippers, but in Washington there were Colored women in pastel crepe and linen dresses with high heels to match. With their bronzed lips and cornrows, these women held their heads erect and spoke like people on television.

The colonnade of the Lincoln Memorial had thirty-six columns representing the states of the union. The guide told us the nineteen-foot statue was carved from white Georgia marble out of Stone Mountain. Towering above us, Lincoln sat in contemplation, a contrast to park statues of public figures standing in a dictatorial manner. The Gettysburg Address and the second Inaugural Address, carved on massive stone tablets, reminded us that "It may seem strange that any man should dare to ask a just God's assistance in wringing their bread from the sweat of other men's faces; but let us judge not, that we be not judged."

Later we went to Ford's Theater and saw the box where the President sat with his wife before John Wilkes Booth shot him. Booth and his eight accomplices thought Lincoln was too lenient in letting Southern states back in the Union even if they abolished slavery and took an oath of allegiance to the United States of America. It seemed to me that Booth didn't know the Golden Rule.

In the Smithsonian, on the same floor as the great recon-structed Tyrannosaurus Rex, was Lincoln's death mask. Pho-tographs of wounded boys treated without sterilization, their wounds infected with "laudable pus," thought to be a good sign giving off "miasmic odors," hung on the walls. Six hundred thou-sand Southern men were killed and at least a million wounded on both sides. Then I saw documents and pictures of the prison camp at Andersonville, Georgia of the thirty-three thousand Union privates who lived in tents and huts with dirt floors. One hundred and fifty men a day died there, yet my schoolbooks never mentioned Andersonville Prison. How could such treatment of fellow countrymen be justified, and then ignored? I wandered away from the official tour.

In the Division of Radiation and Organisms I saw pickled baby animals and human fetuses in glass jars. Butterflies. Worms. Insects. Reptiles. Mutations. Siamese twins.

Everywhere I turned there were worlds of knowledge about which I knew nothing. The brochure said only one percent of the Smithsonian's inventory was on display.

In the rose-white marble art museum I touched real paint-ings, gazed upon the textures of oil and gesso applied by long-dead hands. Peering into rooms chained off from the public I saw millions of books numbered by the Dewey Decimal System. Seventy-eight million in the Library of Congress. I would never be able to read them all. The rooms were full of whispering voices, songs, letters, admonitions, and utopian dreams.

But then I could not remember how I had gotten there. Which stairs had I climbed? Which way had I turned? I tried to retrace my steps, but no hallway looked familiar. My heart was beating fast; I stumbled on a staircase and bloodied my knees. Windows looked out on the vast, unknown city. Doors marked "Exit" led to more strange rooms—period furniture, vases from China. Dragons. Picture languages I did not understand. I was lost. Where were the dinosaurs? Tears that I did not will welled behind my glasses and ran down my face. I wanted to cry out for help, but if I did, my voice would summon no one. My hands shook. My knees were mush.

Mrs. Wilson, plodding slowly along with her hands cupped under her big stomach, said she had to go up and down the elevators and halls to find me. I was so glad to see her! But I didn't say so.

"Young lady, if you wander away again," she told me, "I will make you stay on that hot bus alone. God forbid I should have a child like you who won't follow directions and do like the others."

My classmates were tired and already in their seats. As I boarded the bus and we headed across the Potomac, I felt as if something terrible was going to happen to me. I could just feel it.

Next, our bus drove to Virginia, but we were late because of me and didn't get off the bus to see George Washington's or Thomas Jefferson's plantations. In the Arlington National Cemetery, land originally part of Robert E. Lee's plantation, the head stones of Confederates were pointed so Yankees could not sit on them. It was unsettling enough to see all those graves, but it somehow seemed worse as we drove past the 29 acres of the Pentagon, the world's largest office building, with the Department of Military Academics that taught the art and history of war.

Mrs. Wilson held tight to seats on either side of her so that she could stand and recite like a tour guide. The boys on the bus turned around and glared at me because they couldn't stop and see the cannon displays in the Pentagon.

"You held your classmates up by getting lost. Can't you do anything right?" said the voice in my head. "Why can't you be like everyone else?"

Returning home to a school without a library was dispiriting. Wishing I had not been found, I longed to live in the Smithsonian. All I needed was a map and a place to sleep.

The Grand Finale

Precariously balancing a stack of seventh grade books under one arm while gripping my old brown suitcase held shut with black elastic, I paused to lean the heap of books on a parked car in front of a house where three little girls hung onto the wrought iron banisters of the front steps. I waved at them because they were always there, looking for something, their faces tucked behind one another. I passed their house every afternoon on my way to help Mr. Leitzsey with his beginners' dance classes. I made $1.25 an hour. Today was important because the dance recital was tonight.

Straightening the uneven load, I hurried up the hill ahead to where I rewarded myself with a low-hanging white dogwood blossom I stuck behind my ear. I had learned something about walking two miles from a Sunday school lesson. If I kept my eye on a certain mailbox until I got to it, and then made my next goal a blue parked car, then a dogwood tree, my walk would seem shorter, and I wouldn't get tired. Of course, the lesson was about living a Christian life, but I used it anyway. I also kept the rhyme "Keep a -goin'" by Frank L. Stanton, the poet laureate of Georgia. It played in my head while I stepped to its beat:

If you strike a thorn or rose, keep a-goin'! If it hails or if it snows, keep a-goin'!

Riding past me in a silver jacket and a space helmet, a boy on a bicycle pedaled fast up the hill, and as he turned his head to watch me, he ran his bike into the curb.

"Hey, girl, watch where you're going!"

"Watch yourself!" I shot back. "I know where I'm going."

The boy, with one hand clamped on his space helmet, picked up his bicycle. I hated the way all the boys and the teachers at school were so intent on being astronauts to catch up with the Russians. He might be a charming prince, I thought, if he'd studied Russian ballet. I held out one arm with a curved hand as though inviting him to take it, but instead retraced my steps to pick up books I had dropped and started down the stretch of street to the dance studio.

J. Frank Leitzsey's Dance Studio was a triangular green brick building with dark green vines and pink dancers painted on the front windows. Unlocking the studio door, I stepped into the Friday afternoon light as it struck the glass panels lining the classrooms to reveal all the mothers' nose prints on the outside and the students' handprints on the inside. The desk where Mrs. Flo Leitzsey sat, with her bobbed black hair and pink-circle-rouged cheeks, was empty except for the receipt book. I turned on the lights in the hot and dusty studio. The exercise bars, which had pulled out of the walls last Christmas, were still tied up with the long cords Mr. Leitzsey has used. "Necessity is the mother of intervention," he had said of his rigging, but because I was only his helper, I hadn't corrected him.

Being his assistant was the best way to learn the craft, he had said, and I liked demonstrating the steps while he played on the piano and counted, "one-and-two-and- lift-and-point." Walking down the rows of girls, I would pass my hand under bent fingers to extend the curve, move in now and then to push the stiff girl with pig tails down the bar in a painful extension while turning her hips out. I straightened backs, always watching the lines of movement, trying to make the girls feel it, but every so often a tear would slide down a flushed cheek.

Besides playing the piano, Mr. Leitzsey organized the class themes, costumes, and recital plans, yet he was forever picking the sloppiest students to do a hula for the veterans or making me perform a dance in toe shoes in a funny clown costume for the Elks Club when what I wanted was to be was the Sugar Plum Fairy. His wife loved to pass out colored band-aids to the beginning pointe class when their first blisters popped, but I wanted to tell them how Pavlova had danced the last movement of *Swan Lake* leaving trails of blood on the floor.

The record player and the piano had already been taken to Joe E. Brown High, named for the Governor who had served four terms. And called Jefferson Davis a tyrant. I checked the dressing room to make sure that all the costumes had been taken. I put my faded pink pointe shoes in the brown suitcase. I left my books on a bench in the dressing room and lifted the monstrous papier-mâché head. Mr. Leitzsey had crafted it for the recital using the head of a reindeer sculpture that had previously graced his front yard at Christmas to create the head of a crow. There was no grace in this creation. While the antlers of the reindeer made the head taller and wider than normal, it did help emphasize the "scare" in scarecrow.

Slipping the head on, I clicked off the lights in the back of the studio and felt my way into the classroom. I nodded my head from side to side, crooking my arms. Someday it would come to Mr. Leitzsey that a scarecrow didn't have the head of a crow, but of a farmer who *scared* the crows. I adjusted the holes so that my eyes looked back at me from the black feathered head reflected in the long mirrors on the walls of the studio. No proper dancer had ever had to wear such an ugly costume. I made little hippity hops forward and low circling swoops back again and long sliding sweeps to each side flapping my imaginary wings.

Then, in the mirror, I caught sight of the line of my graceful movements—the extended crow's beak continued by an extended leg and outstretched arms. Not romantic, no. But striking, perhaps even beautiful. And then it came to me. A leap! A sudden leap at the end. As soon as all the little crows had finished dancing around me and had caught the scarecrow, I would leap straight up and pause like Nijinsky had done with Karsavina. It would be a grand finale. I took off the black head, turned off the lights and started for the high school auditorium. Two blocks away, cars loaded with costumes and dancing shoes waited.

Both of my parents worked and went to night school. My stepfather had an accounting exam tonight and we had only one car so my mother wouldn't be able to see me either. I didn't mind that they didn't understand how important dancing was to me. They thought it was only to make me graceful and to keep me busy every afternoon until they got home.

Ahead of me in the auditorium parking lot, a grandmother with needles, pins, and thimble was still fitting a bright taffeta skirt to a skipping little girl.

"Miss Bonnie Belle is my ballet teacher," Sue Ann whispered to her grandmother. I took pleasure in being called "Miss Bonnie Belle." Sue Ann was one of the little crows in the last number and had good technique when she wasn't jumping around or making trouble.

I carried my costume up the steps to the scratched maroon doors of the auditorium. This certainly wasn't the Mariinsky Theatre in Moscow! If I were a star there, I would only have to say, "Bonnie Belle," and a doorman with admiration in his eyes would part the theatre doors for me. Inside this lobby, Junior League members set up the Coke stand for intermission, while a baldheaded man in a Junior Civitan shirt was crawling out from behind the popcorn machine. Mr. Leitzsey had already hung up his sign across the entrance: "Frank and Flo Leitzsey Welcome You to the 1955 Spring Fling. Enrollments for Fall Class begin August 13th."

I walked through the double doors in time to see Mr. Leitzsey bang on the piano, pull at his thinning hair, and scream for Flo to come quickly.

"The turntable won't turn, the lights won't light, and the costumes aren't finished!" he fretted. "Plus, Sue Ann's grandmother wants to pay for last month's lessons, and she wants a receipt. Bonnie Belle told her to see you."

Flo Leitzsey gave him a "now, Frank, honey" pat and took Sue Ann's grandmother backstage. I went to the lobby, bought a Coke, and took it down to the piano for Mr. Leitzsey.

"Thank God you're here," he said, turning to pull me to him.

I realized for the first time that all the sweat and dust that I associated with dancing class belonged solely to Mr. Leitzsey's purple silk shirt, which I had never seen him without.

"Get backstage and see if you can get the dancers in line," he instructed me, crunching around a mouthful of ice and pulling at the sides of his grey-streaked hair. "And give out the hats and canes for the first number. And watch Fatty Patty. She might throw up if her mama's around."

I ran up the stairs, pausing long enough for a quick hug to Mrs. Leitzsey's lavender scented bosom, then to the dressing room, where the day before the varsity basketball players had won the city championship. Already the black and white tiles were covered with red bows, powder, and glitter. Choosing a shower stall away from the older girls, I draped my pink and white tutu, checkered tap costume, and black crow wings across the door to claim it as my own private dressing room. I pulled on my practice leotard and tights. Outside the dressing room, with my hand on the sink for a bar, I sank down in deep pliés.

I spent the afternoon of the rehearsal lining up dancers, sorting out turquoise and yellow Japanese paper parasols, hair ribbons and tap-shoe bows, while castanet and tambourine rhythms played around me. When Mr. Leitzsey screamed at Mrs. Leitzsey, I brought him another Coca- Cola. I already felt tired and scared about the last number, the leap. And then there were two incidents that I knew wouldn't have happened if I had been appearing with a professional troupe.

The first was the image the photographer had taken. Two weeks ago, when the photos were taken, I had worn a pink and white tutu on which I had sewn thirty-five graduated ruffles under the two rows of ruffles that Mr. Leitzsey thought sufficient. I had practiced and practiced the high arabesque that Karsavina used in her most lovely pictures, and I had borrowed eyeliner from another girl's mother to line my eyes and add subtle wings in the corners. As a final perfect touch, I put a beauty spot just above the left corner of my lips. The photographer had delivered the pictures in a brown envelope with "to be remade" scribbled across the front. I removed the photograph and saw that my pose, the long, graceful arabesque, made me look like a Rector Set model about to fall over. My two black eyes were set in a wide-open stare, and the beauty spot had blurred and doubled when the camera snapped on my stumble. I pushed the photograph back into the brown envelope.

The second bad thing was that I was late getting on stage for the final practice of the Crow's Dance, but I blame Sue Ann for that because she caused an uproar backstage when she caught a spider and presented it to her grandmother. When Mr. Leitzsey started yelling my name, I knew I had spent too much time back-stage trying to undo the spider chaos.

"Where is the scarecrow? How can the show get on the road if the rehearsal never gets off the road?" I finally arrived on stage, having had trouble getting the crow's head to sit properly on my shoulders.

Before Mr. Leitzsey could say more, I positioned myself on the scarecrow's stand, my head hanging to one side, my feathered arms crooked over the edges of the wooden crosspiece. I hung there motionless.

The music, Mr. Leitzsey's own rendition of "Turkey in the Straw" began, and the two beginner pointe classes of little black crows danced out onstage in double lines from both wings, alter-nating back and forth on the chorus. Then I did my part and turned around and called the crows to gather round. They did it perfectly; I had taught them the movement that the swans make in *Swan Lake* when they first see the queen. As the little crows formed a circle around me, I began tilting my head side to side with the music. Then I swung out one leg and lifted my arms off the cross. The crows scooted back up stage and then I danced alone.

We practiced again and again, but I kept my finale plan a secret. When it was finally time for the performance, I remem-bered every step, all the funny kicks and tricks that Mr. Leitzsey had taught me. I fell to my knees like a stupid, clumsy clown; I rolled over and over like an acrobat; and I dangled my hands from the ends of my straight arms like a real scarecrow. The audi-ence laughed and laughed, but soon they would be applauding for something more glorious than these vaudeville tricks.

It was nearing the end, and I was now crouched on the ground. The little crows had tormented me into submission. As planned, they joined arms around me and danced in a moving circle. In and out, they pointed their toes. They were too close. I could barely see their movements through the papier-mâché eye holes, but I sensed the movements were awkward and ugly. The little crows rushed forward and raised their arms so the scarecrow could now rise, at first unseen by the audience. Their bent knees and heels jabbed me in the side. The toe of someone's shoe pushed at the front of the scarecrow's head. Now upright, I expected to see again the bright lights of the stage for the final scene, but inside the head, all was black.

Mr. Leitzsey made a crescendo run on the piano and the crows pulled me up by the arms. Together they danced in a single line, following me. I paused, and the crows danced alone on one side of the stage leaving me to prepare for my series of turns around them that would scare them out of the field of green and yellow crepe paper cornstalks. I began to twirl and felt with each turn the counterbalance of the heavy scarecrow's head as it moved in the opposite direction to my own. The audience roared with laughter, and the doors in the back of the auditorium, where tired parents always disappeared after their own child's number, had stopped swinging. I had to do it now. Even the crows, tiptoeing in fright, were laughing at the turned-around head.

Now!

I breathed in deep, my heart pounding in my chest. I felt the leap beginning in my legs and everything seemed to slow down as my body lifted into the air, high above the heads of the awkward little crows. Above, it felt as if the air had been stripped away, leaving only the bright, bright lights. For one moment, I was Nijinsky, lifting in the air, unbound to anything like what fettered my parents to their relentless working or what kept boys on bikes from seeing beauty dancing before them. But the moment was fleeting. Like a body walking in the sun too long, my arms and legs wouldn't quite work together. Straining to hold my front leg up high and I pointed, I pushed too far forward and on the way down, it seemed that I had been up higher than even Nijinsky.

The music had stopped.

I had leapt off the stage, one foot brushing the top of the piano, and Mr. Leitzsey, ever impeccable in his timing, caught me in his arms.

We both sprawled on the gym floor. He pulled off the crow's head and wiped my face on his purple shirt. The audience clapped, laughed, and applauded. Mr. Leitzsey stood and bowed.

"God help us, that was a grand finale, Miss Bonnie Belle," he said with that vaudeville twinkle in his eyes. "A grand finale."

Taking a quick bow, I hurried back to the dressing room before the others arrived. My mother and stepfather, who had arrived late, just in time for my leap, were backstage.

"That was a real cute ending," said my mother.

"This girl's a real hoofer," said my stepfather.

I hated them because they didn't know what I had tried to accomplish. Before my parents tried to shepherd me into the car, I went back to the gym to pick up my schoolbooks and saw the ugly locker room covered with love-and-kill graffiti. As we drove home, I saw out the back window a dogwood tree at the top of the hill illuminated by a streetlamp. I imagined myself there, looking down on the auditorium and the stage and the lights, and what the final leap would be like in a real theatre.

Flood in Louisiana

Aunt Marty started to wring her freckled hands as soon as she saw the evening news. Hurricane Audrey, a category 4, had struck southwest Louisiana and already 350 people were dead. Water was up to the treetops, and families were squatting on pitched roofs in hopes of being rescued. My aunt's married daughter Maribel was living in Louisiana near the naval base.

It was the hot, still end of June and we were in a room at the Good Times Motel on our way from Atlanta, Georgia to West Palm Beach, Florida, where Aunt Marty and Uncle Oscar lived with their son, my cousin Mikey. He and I were both thirteen years old, so my parents said that soon we'd be too old to take vacations together and sleep in the same bed to save money.

One thing Mikey and I had in common was that we thought our mothers would drive us crazy if we didn't ignore them most of the time. They were so intent on us making something of ourselves in the future that they didn't like us in the present. This was especially true of my mother, who had been the first daughter to leave the farm, graduate from high school in the city, and go to business college. My grandfather on my mother's side died early, so my mother and Aunt Marty clung together. Eventually, they had children with me and Mikey—sharing the exact same birthday.

And Mikey and I had seen each other naked. There was a peephole in Mikey's bathroom around an electrical outlet that had been installed by Uncle Oscar. We looked at each other through that peephole without either of us ever acknowledging the deed out loud. Mikey's wiener got bigger whenever he knew I was looking.

"I knew it!" Aunt Marty said. "I knew when Maribel left home something horrible would happen. My beautiful girl is gone, gone! First, she gave up her career and married a louse. And now she's drowning!"

A champion roller skater since the age of eight, Maribel was a beautiful blonde with a year-round tan. Aunt Marty had made tight-fitting satin outfits with short sequined skirts for her and entered her into all the contests she could find so that their house was covered with photographs of Maribel holding flowers or trophies. Aunt Marty had used makeup to make Maribel look a lot older than she was, so Maribel started pairs skating before she was a teenager and started dating before she was sixteen. I, on the other hand, had what people remarked was a friendly, pleasant face. I had to wear glasses, I wasn't allowed to wear lipstick, and my mother had given me a Toni home permanent, so my hair was dry and frizzy.

Uncle Oscar, shining his shoes with the motel's shoe wipes, said that Aunt Marty shouldn't worry until she knew she had something to worry about. Aunt Marty said she was going to call Maribel, but when she dialed, the operator said she couldn't get through.

"We've got to call the Red Cross," Aunt Marty told Oscar.

"No, we don't," Uncle Oscar said. "Maribel's probably been evacuated to the naval base. Surely, they know what to do with a little water. And besides, the government isn't going to let anything happen to their boys."

Aunt Marty stayed up all night, worrying. Mikey and I slept together on the pull-out couch. Since the previous summer, Mikey had grown hair on his legs. Uncle Oscar was snoring in the double bed, alone. Aunt Marty sat by the window with the drapes open so that she could see the phone by the neon lights from the parking lot. It seemed to me that every twenty minutes she picked it up and dialed, but each time the operator couldn't put her through. I watched her silhouette, cut out of the darkness, and framed against the neon-lit window, until my eyes closed, and my ears took over the surveillance. Eventually, I fell asleep. The next morning, Aunt Marty was slumped in the chair with the phone resting on her stomach and the receiver dangling.

We took turns in the bathroom washing up and getting dressed before we walked to the coffee shop next door and, except for Aunt Marty, ate heartily. I had cheese grits, scrambled eggs, and ham with red-eye gravy. After breakfast, we packed up our belongings, including the Monopoly game that Mikey and I had played the night before. He and I kept a list of our separate assets so that we could open the board at any time and continue playing. We'd been playing Monopoly together since we were seven years old.

When he was little, Mikey didn't play outside because he had breathed in the smoke from burning poison oak, causing all his insides to swell and blister. For three years, he lived on thin oatmeal and soft rice. I spent those summers reading and playing games with him, and in the seasons between I wrote entertaining letters to him.

Now, you couldn't tell that anything had ever been wrong with Mikey. He was taller than me but still towheaded, his hair so light in color that from a distance it looked like a halo. His warm brown eyes appealed to me as if he were a puppy who wanted to be patted or taken for a walk. He told me that I was his only true friend, and I used to think I'd marry him when we grew up, even though I knew that first cousins weren't supposed to have children together because they'd get a freak.

On the highway, we stopped at every roadside market so that Aunt Marty could try to call Maribel. First came the signs advertising pecan pralines and then the displays of coconut heads with seashell faces hanging by long tufts of hair from the roof braces of outdoor stalls, like the scalps of monkeys swinging in the warm breeze. I thought they were disgusting, so I was embarrassed to even go into those places, but Aunt Marty begged Uncle Oscar to stop at each one. Sometimes we got big orange drinks and pralines and used the public restrooms.

Uncle Oscar waited for us in front of the revolving stands of postcards, watching the young girls in their shorts and halters. He was good at striking up conversations with young people, but in the car with all of us, though, he had very little to say. Sometimes in the summers he drove Mikey and me to the movies, singing all the way there. He wore brown and white shoes, which were always polished, and he told jokes and kidded us a lot—but never when Aunt Marty was around.

"Cut the foolishness, Oscar," she would reprimand him.

When we stopped in Albany, Georgia, I went to the restroom and discovered a spot of "it." It was just a little bit of red in my underwear. I hoped I might have somehow gotten hurt without feeling any pain. I knew all about getting periods, because I'd read a book my mother sent for called *How to Tell Your Daughter*, but I just didn't think "it" would happen to me when I was away from home.

We decided to eat some lunch. I had fried catfish, hush puppies, coleslaw, and iced tea. My mother wouldn't let me eat fried food at home because she said my face would break out in awful pimples. Uncle Oscar had catfish, too. He pitched his hush puppies into the air, howled like a hound, and then caught them in his mouth.

"How can you carry on at a time like this?" Aunt Marty wailed at him.

"Because it's the kids' vacation. Your worrying never saved a soul."

"Don't you talk about souls to me, Oscar," she said. "Yours hasn't been anywhere to get saved."

In West Palm Beach, Aunt Marty always went to the Church of God, but although Uncle Oscar might drive Mikey and me to Sunday school, he never went in, preferring to stand outside and talk or drive to the corner drugstore and start a conversation with someone at the soda fountain.

After we ate lunch, we went to the restrooms one more time before hitting the road. My red spot was bigger. Everyone always said that "it" caused stomach cramps and headaches, but I didn't hurt anywhere. I rolled up some toilet paper to make a pad and looked for Aunt Marty, but she wasn't in the restroom. When I got outside, I saw her at the pay phone with tears in her eyes. She told me she still wasn't getting through to Maribel. I wondered whether I was turning into a hemophiliac. I decided not to say anything to Aunt Marty because she had enough to worry about, but I was careful not to bruise myself. I thought we'd stop for the night somewhere and then I could ask Aunt Marty what she thought was wrong with me, but as soon as we were in the car again, Aunt Marty persuaded Uncle Oscar to drive straight through to their house so that she could be where Maribel might call her.

"My baby knows her mother is worried," she said. "That sergeant of hers is no good. I knew he'd get my darling in a fix. Next thing you know, she'll be pregnant and lose her figure."

"I don't think Maribel will let that happen," Uncle Oscar said. "Plus, I'm worried about the immediate situation, Marty,"

"Please, Jesus! Save Maribel from the flood!"

In the backseat, I tried to sit very still, believing that if my body didn't move, nothing would happen. Monthly periods couldn't be mentioned in front of men. My stepfather wouldn't even buy tampons for my mother at the store. If something else was wrong, if I were dying of something, I reasoned, it would be better to be in West Palm Beach than on the road. My mother could take a day off from work and come see me in the hospital on my last day.

I was reconciled to the long ride in the car if I lived that long. My legs began to ache. My heart fluttered in my chest. My hands were clammy. I felt chilled. I'd heard that if you wash your hair while you're having your period you get pneumonia. I shivered and folded my arms around my ribs.

Mikey wanted to get out the Monopoly board and play.

I said, "No. I don't feel good."

"Come on. Just 'cause I'm worth more than you are?"

That did it. I agreed to play. The board fit across my lap, and Mikey laid out the bank across the rear window because it was level. He won the dice roll, so he went first, and on that move, he bought some more property.

In the front seat, Aunt Marty started describing Maribel's junior skating championship and told us how the judges had loved her pageboy hairstyle and blossoming figure. I had one now, but no one noticed.

To my surprise, Uncle Oscar said what my mother always said: "You ruined her, Marty." My mother thought that Maribel got exactly what she wanted but never appreciated it.

My mother also blamed Uncle Oscar for not exerting himself when he disagreed with Aunt Marty about what Maribel should be allowed to do.

"Uncle Oscar doesn't have any backbone," Mama said.

Meanwhile in the backseat, I wasn't doing well at Monopoly. I went to jail and didn't collect $200. I was stuck in jail for eight more turns, but I didn't really care. I could feel the pad that I had made swelling up with blood like a big country tick. I wanted to keep the game board on my lap, but I feared that the game would end soon. I was running out of money, I wasn't concentrating on the game, and I felt ashamed and alone. I wished I were at home. Although Mama would be at work now, I could go to the bathroom and open the box of sanitary napkins that she'd bought for me. That's how she would find out that I'd gotten "it." I always had trouble talking to her about personal things. She had the same trouble, I think.

When we crossed the Florida state line after midnight and pulled into Jacksonville, I said I wasn't hungry and I wanted to stay in the car. Really, I didn't want anyone to see me. I was afraid there might be a giant stain on the back of my shorts.

"Well, we can't leave you in the car," Uncle Oscar said. "You might get kidnapped."

Mikey said he wanted a hamburger and that I was too old to get kidnapped. Uncle Oscar said he needed to stretch his legs for a bit, so he got out of the car, walked all the way into the diner, shaking his head as he went.

"You're no fun!" Mikey yelled at my window before he joined his father in the diner.

Aunt Marty told me to cooperate because she had to call Maribel again and didn't want me sitting alone in the car in a strange town.

"Something is happening to me!" I sobbed.

"What is it, honey?" Aunt Marty asked, reaching through the open window to lay her hand on my trembling shoulders. "Are you sick?"

I nodded.

"Well, whereabouts?"

"Down there," I said quietly between sobs. "I'm bleeding to death!"

"Lordy, you've just got 'the curse.' Now you're a woman, and you'll just have to put up with cramps, men, childbirth, and then hot flashes," she said. "You've reached the age of accountability. You can now go to Hell if you break a commandment."

"Aunt Marty, I don't have any sanitary napkins."

"All the stores are closed this time of night," she said. "Why, when I was a young girl, all we had were clean, old rags."

She told me to lie down and that she'd bring me back a Coca Cola to sip and get me some towels out of the trunk, but I didn't really feel sick. I was scared. I was still holding the Monopoly board because Mikey and I had been playing by flashlight for the last three hundred miles with Mikey loaning me money at four percent interest.

When my aunt locked the doors, I was grateful to be alone. I could smell myself, like the pail of cut-up fish that Uncle Oscar had caught at Fernandina Beach. I hoped that Aunt Marty wouldn't tell Uncle Oscar that I'd gotten my period.

A truck pulled into the parking lot with its bed full of baying hounds who barked and moaned at me. I could see the neon lights blinking BILLIE MAE'S COFFEE HOP, because the S no longer worked. A boy and a girl were kissing in a car. A very pregnant woman with her husband's hand at her back stepped out of the diner. He opened the door for her, nudging the edge of her skirt inside the car with care, as if she were a china doll.

I woke up when I heard a key in the trunk. A moment later, Aunt Marty was banging at my window.

"Here you go," she said, handing me a towel and an old blouse of hers.

I pushed the towel inside the leg of my shorts and the blouse underneath me. The towel, one Uncle Oscar used to wipe off his car, was stiff and rough. He kept his car as polished as his shoes.

When they all came back to the car, Aunt Marty said that she still hadn't gotten an answer from Maribel but that the phone lines were working again.

"Jesus will save my Maribel, my precious girl!"

Then without any warning, she announced to Uncle Oscar and Mikey that I was "on the rag," that I had "female problems."

I felt dirty and sick. I wished I were on Mars—anywhere but in this car.

Mikey said he didn't want to play Monopoly anymore. He put away the money and cards without tallying our real estate, and then moved away from me and leaned against his door, leaving the board on my lap. Uncle Oscar turned on the car radio softly, and we rode for a long time without conversation. I fell asleep.

When I woke up, the sun was coming up and Mikey was slumped against his door.

"Lord, hear my call and protect her," Aunt Marty prayed softly, over and over.

For a moment, I thought she was talking about me, but she wasn't. I was beginning to wish that Maribel had drowned. As long as it was quick. I raised my thighs, pushing up against the Monopoly board, pointed my toes, and stretched my arms so that my elbows were up next to my ears. Palm trees lined the highway. We were deep into Florida.

Finally, we reached West Palm Beach. As soon we pulled into the driveway, Aunt Marty jumped out of the car before it had stopped. The front door flung open, and then Maribel was standing there in a pretty orange sundress. Aunt Marty hugged her over and over again, what seemed like at least a hundred times.

"My Maribel's home! She's home! Why didn't you answer the phone?"

"I was busy, Mama, saving my clothes and makeup from the dirty water."

Everyone except me bolted out of the car, ran up the front steps, and disappeared into the house. Nobody noticed that I was still in the car. I knew that I had to get inside before Uncle Oscar came back to get the suitcases. I rose, and the red-splotched towel slipped to the floor. I rolled it up under my arm and folded Aunt Marty's blouse, wedged it between my legs, and moved carefully. When I had made it up the front steps, I saw Aunt Marty kneeling in the living room, thanking and praising Jesus.

"Put your bloody rags in the tub in cold water to soak," she said, raising her head to look at me.

I headed straight for the bathroom, but Maribel stopped me in the hallway.

"Bonnie," she said, "I heard you had your own flood. You sure are starting early."

"I'm twelve going on thirteen," I said, pushing past her to step into the bathroom.

"You have no reason to cry," she said. "Your fun days are just beginning. Don't you have any sanitary pads? I only have tampons but let me spray my hair and I'll go get you what you need."

Mikey was standing in the hallway outside the bathroom. He glanced at me but then turned his eyes away. I closed the door. In the bathroom mirror, I didn't look any different, but my insides felt as if they were pushing down to my knees. A period gets rid of old stuff in the stomach, I'd read. I sat on the toilet and waited for Maribel.

'Twixt and 'Tween

I hadn't even complained out loud about my life, but I was somehow guilty of insolence because of an elusive "attitude" that Mama could see coming. Teen-agers could cause mothers to have nervous breakdowns. My friends, whose mothers had breakdowns, said the afflicted screamed at husbands and children and cried a lot about being taken for granted. Sometimes they sweated in the winter and shivered in the summer. Sometimes they stayed in their bedrooms and refused to do the washing and cooking. Sometimes their hands shook and their lips quivered. It occurred to me that my mother was protecting herself from a nervous breakdown by sending me away for the summer.

She said it was time for me to leave Atlanta and go visiting, so in the summer of my thirteenth year, I didn't go to Camp Calvin or to work part-time at Leitzsey's tap-dance studio. Instead, I was to spend two weeks with my mother's parents on the farm in Henry County; two weeks with the widow, Great Aunt Alice; and then four weeks with my Grandmother Henderson's cousins in Athens, Georgia. I couldn't spend time with my real father's parents, because my Granny Henderson already lived with us and her husband had disappeared when her two boys had been little. The worst thing of all was that I wasn't allowed to take any books with me.

On my grandparents' small farm, I slept in the bedroom at the long end of the hallway. The iron bedstead sat high off the floor to accommodate the slop jar tucked under the foot. The stern faces and unblinking eyes of unknown relatives stared from oval frames that hung by dusty gold cords and tassels from the picture frame moulding. The top drawer of the dresser held faded tintypes of twin girls who had died in a fire. Bibles, Farmer's Almanacs, and crochet patterns were the only things to read in that house.

Little Granny, Cynthia LaMaude Benefield Johnson, whose father, Hiram, served in the House of Representatives, married Grandpa when she was only 15 and he was 24. She had five children who lived. After Grandpa couldn't make a good living for the family, she brought in money by lining tiny coffins with satin and tatting for babies who died when they were born. Where she couldn't buy, she bartered her quilts to chiropractors and traveling salesmen who could get coffee and holiday presents for her children. In farming communities, people always gave what was left of cutting up a pig or fabric from curtains or extra corn or cough medicine after their child got well to whomever needed it. During the Depression, there were no breadlines in Henry County, named for Patrick Henry.

When I got to the farm, she asked me whether I had a sweetheart.

"No," I said.

"When you get one," she said, "don't let him give you too many babies."

My job was to dig up peanuts and sweet potatoes while Grandpa, John Lowry Johnson, plowed the field with his mule, Ole Red. Sometimes he plowed the same furrow twice. My job wasn't really hard work, so I could spend the hours imagining other places. The only hard part was that Grandpa had a rule that my knees couldn't touch the ground unless I was praying.

Leaning over in the hot sun made me dizzy, and though I earnestly tried to pray, concentration on holy thoughts didn't come easy for me. My mind wandered off, wondering what my girlfriends Jenny and Carolyn were doing back in Atlanta.

Sometimes Grandpa caught me "praying" in my head but not moving my lips.

"Watch now," he warned, pointing his index finger at me. "If the devil gets an inch in your head, he'll take a mile."

This didn't make sense, even if that length of evil was curled up to fit in my head. Regardless, I would quickly recite the Lord's Prayer or Psalm 23 or Paul's treatise on love from 1 Corinthians. Anything.

One evening after sunset, Grandpa and I went looking for a cow that had wandered out of the pasture. On the rise of the hill where some of his past mules had been buried, Grandpa began to sing "Listen to the Mockingbird," his camp-meeting voice faltering on the chorus. Most of the words were lost in evening breeze and the verses I did hear made no sense to me.

I shouldn't have expected anything he said to make logical sense. When Mama had been little, he'd fallen into a well while surveying, bashed the back of his head, broke his ribs and lower legs, and lay unconscious for more than a week before the searchers found him. After he was rescued, Grandpa was recognized as a lay preacher full of the Holy Spirit because he knew the Book of Revelation by heart. "Oh! Listen ye, daughter of Zion. The harps are hung on the trees. The weary winds are wearily moaning. I am resolved . . . say it after me. I am resolved no longer to linger, charmed by the world's delights."

"I am resolved to be charmed by the world's delights," I recited.

He placed his rough hand on my head, and his sweat spread out over my hair.

"Your mockingbird will sing to you in the dark," he said. The ballad was about a mockingbird singing over the grave of a man's sweetheart when he comes home from the war. I wanted that bird to stay in the trees away from me. "The owl will be watching you when you come to the Age of Accountability."

I was already thirteen and still, no one would let me be accountable for anything. I had no choices, not even the choice to sin. They just let me be guilty.

One day we walked down the gravel road to a Colored family who took in washing and ironing. Grandpa let them live there and when he died, the land would become theirs. Young children carried loads of wood to fuel the fire for the boiling pots. Grandpa handed our wash to a woman he called Alfasia, and I helped to lay washed overalls and blankets on rocks in the sun. When I saw that Grandpa was jawing with Alfasia's husband, I went behind the shack with the oldest girl, Geneva, and read comic books, careful to not get red dye from the newsprint on me. Whenever Grandpa saw red paint on someone, like nail polish, he proclaimed that the devil had hit the person with his hammer. It seemed to me that if the devil hated me enough to smash my fingers, then I must be good.

Later that night, he yanked me by the arm out of bed. I was barely awake, yet I could see that his other hand held switches cut from a hickory tree. The switches stung my legs like firebrands as he whipped me. I yelled out for help, but Little Granny never came.

"What did I do?" I kept asking Grandpa. "What did I do?"

"You sneaked and looked at the devil words of Alfasia's brat with the mark of Cain. The likes of her bear the curse of Ham."

"Well I'm a brat too, but I'm not poor," I told him, adding. "And I don't have dark skin."

My scalded, wet feelings were knotted inside my fists. I demanded to know why he had not scolded or whipped me in Alfasia's yard.

"Why are you waking me up now?" I asked.

"Because you wouldn't remember in the dark where the whelps had come from," he told me, "but you'll remember what they'd been for."

I never forgot either one.

Back under the bedcovers, I cried—not for myself but for my mother. She told me that her uncle, who would stand closest to the fireplace while the children were pushed back, once grabbed the little patch of hair that grew on the back of her neck. He shouted out, "Where did you get this one, Maude? You oughta throw her back in the fire," and everyone laughed. At my age, Mama had run away from the farm, somehow gone to Atlanta, and lived with Captain and Mrs. Robbins of the Salvation Army so she could go to Russell High School. She learned to play a trumpet, wore the Army bonnet, graduated, went to Atlanta Secretarial School while working for the Army in their affordable clothes store, and got a good job at the telephone company. In all the churches Mama had experienced, the most well off men were in charge of everything. The Salvation Army welcomed women, youth, poor people, and those of every skin shade to all wear the same uniform, carry a fisherman's kettle, and ring the bells. When Grandpa was no longer invited to preach at the Noah's Ark church his daddy had founded, he called on the smoked hams hanging in the smokehouse to turn from their sinful ways and be born into everlasting gladness.

Great Aunt Alice was the most admired woman in my mother's family. At her house, I slept in the Lillian Russell bedroom, whose cherry wood bed had six layers of embroidered sheets, blankets, blanket covers, ruffled bed slip, and a pink taffeta bedspread with a covering of crochet medallions. Two drawers of the dresser contained only lace handkerchiefs scented with lavender and rose. The bottom drawer contained folded, ironed pillowcases, each embroidered with antebellum ladies whose petticoats formed the edge of the case, outlined in variegated pastel colors of tatting. Corset covers nestled neatly in the same drawer.

Aunt Alice's storybook house had a parlor in which we spent the day and evening hours. Except for a short trip down three back stairs in the morning to cut flowers for the table, Aunt Alice never went outside.

"The sun is bad for the skin," she said.

Aunt Alice's white hair waved over her porcelain forehead. Her complexion was the color of my mama's white cold cream, her rouged cheeks shaped like open rose petals. She was Little Granny's older sister, a widow.

Great Uncle Robert's framed picture stood on the mantel, along with his Bible, his gold pocket watch, and the last handkerchief he'd carried. Whenever she crossed the room or said his name, Aunt Alice always nodded at his picture.

Aunt Alice taught me how to make tea cakes, black bottom pie, and divinity. Except for sugar-cured ham, sent to her by Senator Eugene Talmadge, Aunt Alice didn't eat meat. I don't think she'd ever had a hamburger. As for the sweets, we ate most of them ourselves, but when Aunt Alice became tired of desserts, she called her neighbors, told them she'd baked something special for them, and asked them to come fetch it. Everyone seemed to know they should wait at the front door for Aunt Alice to hand them baked goods that were packaged in small boxes tied with a bow.

"I never let any of them bring their germs into my house," she told me, "and I've never been sick a day in my life."

Even though Aunt Alice didn't know how to drive, Uncle Robert's old black Hudson was parked in the driveway. Every so often, the gas would evaporate from the tank and she would call a man to come fill it up. Her groceries and cough syrup were delivered every Monday morning, and on Wednesdays the bookmobile from the library delivered four novels. The mailman brought her mail to the front door, and the Methodist preacher came to call on Sunday evenings. As soon as he told her the congregational news, he feigned a few coughs and then Aunt Alice offered him a small portion of her cough syrup. She didn't offer me any.

"Why don't you join a garden club, play bridge," I asked her. Aunt Alice didn't have a television or a high-fidelity record player.

"Oh, I'm waiting for your Uncle Robert," she said. "I would never take the chance of missing him by being absent when he comes for me."

For Aunt Alice, Uncle Robert had not died.

"When Robert dies," she once said, "he will have Jesus call me almost immediately so that we can be together."

Since then, she'd decided that her husband would return with Jesus in the Second Coming to drive out Satan and his followers and proclaim His kingdom.

"That's why I keep your Uncle Robert's car in running condition," she said, giving a nod to the mantel.

Aunt Alice said that it was sweet of me to come see her, but I think she was glad when my parents picked me up and drove me away to my next destination.

Grandmother Belle Wallace Henderson's two maiden cousins, Pansy and Maude Ona Moore, lived in a big two-story house with a wraparound porch in Athens, Georgia. Though frail and fair, Pansy designed ball gowns, gave permanent waves, collected butterflies that she framed in burnished gold, and would, by appointment, cut the likenesses of people's heads out of black paper. Pansy's elder sister, Maude, was freckled all over and had uncontrollable henna tinted hair. She had been the first female court reporter in Georgia, and she still penned editorials for three newspapers.

For breakfast, Maude drank mineral oil and ate three bran muffins cooked by Wesley, an old Colored man who had worked for the sisters for many years. Later, she had Wesley mash the pulp of the fruit from their trees to prepare as quarts of sherbet to be stored in the icebox. Except for honey, she didn't allow anyone in the household to eat "sweets." Instead, she served deviled pecans, stuffed dates, and fruit compotes for dessert. She had many bottles of herbs, tea leaves, and tinctures that she ordered from California. Whenever her friends were sick, she made up combinations of these natural medicines, only returning home once they'd swallowed her remedies and promised that they were on the road to recovery.

The worst thing Maude could call anyone was a carpetbagger, an opportunist who'd come South, after General Sherman had burned Atlanta, with the intention of hoodwinking widows by posing as insurance salesmen or coming with promises of eventually returning land and possessions for a monthly fee. If Pansy ever tried telling a story about someone and Maude pronounced the person a carpetbagger or even a friend of a carpetbagger, I never got to hear the end of Pansy's tale.

"All Southern men are weaklings and feebleminded," Maude theorized. "They're the products of the seed of those who were incapable of fighting in the War. All of the good, brave men had been killed on the battlefield.

"But the New South. That was built by women operating behind sorry bankers and politicians. A young Southern woman like you," she said, "can do anything you set your mind to."

Books, pamphlets, and political tracts were stacked in every corner of Maude's side of the house. Her library was peopled with framed sepia photos and tintypes of dead or crippled soldiers. On Pansy's side, her sewing studio had a separate door for access by the public. She let me look through her neatly stacked scrapbooks filled with postcard correspondence so that I could follow the stories by dates, cities, and signatures.

A long fur coat with Hoover buttons still pinned to it functioned as a drape over Maude's chifforobe. The doors were broken off, but there was no telling when that had happened. The hems of the lace curtains in the parlor were shredded, so I helped the sisters to move the curtains from the back of the house to the front and then threaded the brass rods on the kitchen windows through the casings at the tops of old lace petticoats and let them serve as window coverings.

The worst disaster in the house, however, were chunks of ceiling plaster that had fallen on top of Maude's square piano, a mahogany Viennese pianoforte. Its movement was dated 1823. In the evenings, Maude alternated classical works with songs by Stephen Foster. She asked me to play but, without my sheet music or a hymnal, I could play very little.

"I have a bad memory," I said.

"Never say or think that again," she told me. "If you believe anything negative about yourself, it will become true because anything ever thought or known by your mind has existence."

Maude was a member of the International New Thought Alliance. I thought she did some thoughtless, crazy things like bring stray dogs off the back porch and sit them on her piano stool to pound their paws on the keys while she played a melody. She said they were wandering troubadours doing the best they could with what they had.

I was surprised to find in Maude's music cabinet, original lyrics with piano accompaniments penciled in. She had at least fifteen versions of her lullaby explaining to a child the fearful sounds of the night. "To John Doe, Any P.O.," "Dancing Time in Dixie," and "How Much Gold Has the Marigold?" were titles to some of the love songs she'd written. Her favorite piece to play was "'Twixt and 'Tween," a two-step by Otto Krasselt, also of Athens, Georgia. The cover of Krasselt's sheet music bore a photograph of satin-clad slaves strutting in feathered hats. I was certain that their apparent happiness was feigned for the camera. I didn't think slaves in the Old South had fancy satin clothes, property, the right to vote, or to keep their children. Although almost nobody thought anybody should be slaves or unpaid servants anymore, there still didn't seem to be a place for some people. No one wanted to move over. They were still 'twixt and 'tween. And so was I.

I didn't know who I wanted to grow up to be like.

Grandpa Johnson, the head of Mama's family, had climbed Jacob's ladder so high that he no longer made sense to us below. Possessed by the lambasting prophets like those in the Old Testament, mercy and love were missing from his sermons. I didn't want to be his mockingbird, repeating back what it heard. His people founded Noah's Ark Methodist church in Jonesboro and created the cemetery where they were all buried. His daddy was Sheriff of Henry County and then a state representative. My sister and I were invited to come sing "Whispering Hope" at a Noah's Ark homecoming, but we were never asked to bring our "voice of an angel" back again.

Little Granny's work of playing both mother and father since Grandpa's accident, had taken a toll. She was bent over and some days only changed her feed sack apron.

Aunt Alice was a real Southern lady, but she'd lost her own life when Uncle Robert died, leaving her on his stage but without a part.

Maude and Pansy Moore were larger than life in my mind. Maude represented a lineage of individualism that dated back to religious refugees in Nova Scotia, driven out by the British, and banished again on a boat sailing down to Cape Fear in North Carolina. Pansy was a labyrinth of talents and grace. They earned their own livelihood without husbands. My parents had various names for the sisters: kooky, old maids, screwballs, and spinsters. When I left their house loaded down with books, Maude said she'd known that she'd have a daughter someday. I knew that she meant me.

Back home, I began a correspondence with Maude. When other relatives wrote Bible verse notes to me, they might close with, "Be sweet and kiss your mother." Whoever wrote such a note would sign everyone's name to it, as if every member of the household were thinking the same thing, but Maude wrote real letters with crisp details, warm adjectives, and the conflicts of time. Her letters were long, her accounts had beginnings, middles, and ends. She didn't stick Pansy's name at the end, either, as if they experienced the same history in the same way simply by living in the same house and eating at the same table! Sometimes she would include her latest song lyrics so that I could get to know her thinking.

"Go to college," she told me, "learn something besides typing. And get involved in politics."

There She Is,
Miss America

I longed to be Miss America. I had the height, at five foot 8 inches, and the weight, at 125 pounds, but it needed re-arrangement. The perfect Miss America's bust and hips were always equal, the way they were on sewing patterns, with the waist exactly ten inches smaller, like a math formula for what God intended. The women in Georgia must have been obscured beneath kudzu, exchanging recipes when the Creator was imposing that formula because all their hips and thighs were bigger and wider than their bosoms. If I couldn't get my bust bigger with pushups, I'd have to dwindle my hips, so I began in earnest side to side bends, lunges, and scissors-in-the-air exercises. I tried to stand especially straight and to always smile in front of the home economics teachers and, especially, the members of the Chamber of Commerce at my church, hoping they might nominate me for the competition. If I had a great smile like a Miss Congeniality, I hoped the judges would ignore my glasses, the fact that my face was round, not oval, and that my short brown hair was not luxuriously long and silky. Only my Granny thought I was beautiful. My boyfriend said he thought I already had a perfect figure, but he would rather kiss than hear what I thought about anything. I had two years to get ready.

Something about girls strutting and parading about in spike heels and revealing bathing suits seemed not scandalous, but ridiculous. Bathing suits were for swimming and sunning. It would have been more honest to judge the girls naked, or in short see-thru nighties, as the emcee called out their height and weight and printed the measurements of bust, waist, and hip in the program and the city paper, as if they were maidens on an auction block. Perhaps with an extra talent, I could skip the swimsuit competition.

I was my piano teacher's most advanced student, and everyone said I played with expression, which was to say I lacked in technique. While I was most noted for writing winning speeches, from the American Legion oratory contest where I told about the two Washingtons, Booker T. and George, to the play I wrote for Camp Calvin on Jesus' trial with a good attorney, I wouldn't be eloquent in answering Miss America interview questions: "Why do you deserve to win?... What are the four points of a Miss America crown?... Why did you decide to compete?... Where do you see yourself in five years?"

In beautiful pastel evening gowns, before the whole nation, the Miss Americas play violins, perform showy pieces by Chopin on the piano, sing Stephen Foster songs, and dance selections from ballets like *Swan Lake*. When I was 15, Miss Mississippi, Mary Ann Mobley, was crowned Miss America. Bert Parks, the emcee from Atlanta, who sang the same song for 25 years, "There She Is, Miss America," was completely up staged by her formal operatic "Un Bel Di," by Puccini. Midway through the aria, she began peeling off part of her gown as she transitioned into "They'll Be Some Changes Made." After that she was in two movies with Elvis.

It was at church when I was a child and teenager that I got experience reading and speaking and praying in front of an audience. Then strangely, once girls became women, they were expected to be quiet and never seek the limelight. Women were expected to remain silent in meetings; they were not part of decision making with the all-male deacons, elders, or preachers even though all the Sunday school teachers who best knew the Gospel were women. The only executive woman I knew was the first female Superintendent of the Atlanta Public School system, the fastest growing system in the South. Ira Jarrell, a large lady who did not shrink from voicing her opinions, was called a Battle-Ax. I heard teachers call her "I'm a Barrel." And I repeated it.

My mother was afraid I might get lost if I traveled outside Georgia, but if I were Miss America, I could travel to every state and be interviewed on morning TV. If I could be Miss America, I might become a senator or the President of the United States. If I weren't a woman.

Well-Rounded

I never saw my Mama read a book, but she read the *Atlanta Constitution* from cover to cover on Sunday afternoons. Mama and I were avid followers of the comic featuring Brenda Starr, red-headed star reporter. I most loved my mother on those afternoons, for I think it was the only time during her frenetic week that she sat down and did something she enjoyed. Answering my questions with full sentences, she would gaze fondly at her flourishing potted plants and vines stapled across the porch ceiling. The tenseness would disappear from her neck and forehead and her warm olive eyes, set over a square jaw, would smile at me with approval, so I proposed to her that I become a journalist. Smiling, she said working on a paper might be good training for doing newsletters for churches. I vowed then to work on the High School newspaper to please her.

Henderson Chosen for Newspaper Staff as Subfreshman
"An eighth grader, Henderson, agreed to take any unfilled job, begging her way onto the staff of 'The Howl,' the weekly newspaper of Southside High…"

The faculty advisor appointed me as sports photographer. On my first football game assignment, I took fourteen terrific action shots of the wrong team. I redeemed myself with my next piece of prose.

"The Southside football team opened the 1958 campaign with a 33-13 lashing of home-field East Point before 4,000 screaming fans. In the skirmish with West Fulton, the Wolves were held scoreless and to only one first down by the tough Owl defense. Big Bad Wolves growled in their den. They emerged after half time with slobber on their jaws..."

My list of synonyms for winning included maneuvered, scored, assaulted, chalked up, bombarded, pushed, derailed, captured, stunned, and overpowered. Scream, Girls! Victory! Victory!

"In the Southside Talent Show, Bonnie Henderson, daughter of Mr. and Mrs. I. C. Merritt, danced en pointe in her beautiful rendition of the Sugar Plum Fairy choreographed to include a piano solo..."

The principal told my mother that I was sure to look "Well-Rounded" on college applications, and that I might get a scholarship if I kept my activities and grades up.

Henderson Awarded Pillsbury Cook of the Year for Molasses Cookies...

My prize was a stand mixer made by Kitchen Aid that my Mama didn't have room for on her counter. When I tried to make my cookies again, I must have left out an ingredient because they came out flat and black around the edges. Next, I wrote an editorial questioning the educational value of our Home Economics class making sandwiches and cookies every day to take up on the roof where the football team hung out smoking. The faculty adviser shook his head and handed my piece back, but somebody told on me because on the stairs between fifth and sixth period, the star quarterback grabbed me, kissed me hard on the lips, and then tripped me down the steps. My favorite silver and turquoise bracelet broke apart.

"Time Capsule Sealed at Southside High..."

All my unprinted editorials I folded and dropped in an envelope to go into Southside High's time capsule box, a project of the Social Studies Department. I included the one about World History that never moved beyond the Pyramids and another titled, "American History Stopping at The Civil War." We had a solemn ceremony with flags and candles. Many girls cried, believing that when the bomb was dropped, only the time capsule would be left with their memories.

"Henderson's Oration, "Blueprint for Destiny," Wins First Place in the City, the District, the Region, and the State..."

My theme was individual liberty and the common good. The prize was a charm bracelet like Mamie Eisenhower's, with a 14K gold flag. I also received a General Electric puff-bonnet portable hair dryer from the women's auxiliary of the American Legion.

"Henderson Called to Task for Making Size of Photos of the Football Team the Same Size as the Debate Team..."

I was reminded that without community enthusiasm for sports teams, there would not be any advertisers to underwrite printing of the newspaper.

"Henderson Named Singer Seamstress of the Year for Suit with Pill Box Hat..."

My prize was a set of orange Samsonite luggage. By the time I finished the project, the lined straight skirt was too tight.

"Henderson Plans World Religion Series for Youth Group..."

I was Vice President of Y-Teens, Future Teachers of America, Art Club, and Methodist Youth Fellowship. When I invited Mormon missionaries I had met on the bus to come do a Sunday night program for our youth group, the Elders of my church barred the doors and told my stepfather to put me on restriction.

That summer, on hot, sticky evenings when the dogs and lizards would not move to avoid one another, I opened my high school annual to read the inscriptions: "Stay as cute and sweet as you are, and you will go far." The most used was the clever "U R 2 cute 2 B 4 gotten." A five foot nine, big boned girl is not cute and only my Granny thought I was sweet. Why didn't anybody mention the way I ran a meeting, came up with new ideas, or wrote biting and clever editorials? Why would people choose to put in a permanent record words that didn't mean anything? Did language have some other use beyond reporting the truth? When I wrote sweet nothings in others' annuals, what I really meant was "I hope you like me."

What We Did at Elaine Bauman's House

It happened at a New Year's Eve sleepover party on December 31, 1957, when six thirteen-year-old girls, Elaine, Susan, Carolyn, Jenny, Mary Lou, and I, found the composer Rimsky-Korsakov more pleasing than the McGuire Sisters. Elaine Bauman's house in Cascade Heights had authentic paneling with knotholes in the den where we were to stay put for the entire evening.

My parents never went out on holidays because drunks would be swerving all over the road, Mama said. But Mr. and Mrs. Bauman, Elaine's parents, were Episcopalians, so they were going out to celebrate with steaks and alcohol, a ritual that Methodist and strict Presbyterian daughters knew nothing about. Our parents weren't worried about leaving us together for the evening as Jenny, Carolyn, and I were, after all, the smartest and most well behaved girls in the eighth grade. We also were the tallest and sturdiest. In contrast, Susan wore a junior size 5 while we wore Chub-Debs from Sears, Roebuck & Co. Susan also didn't chew her cuticles, and she'd traveled outside Georgia, both north and west.

Elaine had invited Mary Lou to the party as a Christian gesture, even though my mother said that Catholics like Mary Lou weren't Christian because they didn't believe in the Resurrection since Jesus was still on their crucifixes. Mary Lou arrived at the party with Jenny, whose mother picked her up because her father worked the night shift.

Jenny was my best friend outside school. Her mother had real human anatomy books, which she kept on the left end of the bottom shelf in the dining room. She never evaded a question. I'd never known anyone who was divorced, and no one else wore one-piece pantsuits to church, either.

Elaine Bauman had the complete *Encyclopedia Americana* while I had *Compton's Encyclopedia* and only volumes D through F of the *Encyclopedia Britannica*. Elaine's teenage sister had hairdo magazines while I had a younger sister with germs and who chased me with straight pins. Even so, I felt guilty for not including her in my prayers.

When Elaine's parents left for their evening out, we sat cross-legged on the white carpet in the living room instead of in chairs at the kitchen table to paint our sixty fingernails with Revlon's Wild Berry. Mrs. Bauman had said that we weren't to eat or run around on her carpet. My mother thought that proper ladies wore only natural nail polish, and my grandpa said that my fingernails would be ripped out by Satan if I painted them. But there we were, each girl painting her neighbor's nails. Elaine's sister painted Elaine's so that they'd be perfect. Then we took turns reverently placing our hands in the freezer, above the Neapolitan ice cream, to dry. When our nails were dry, we simmered hot chocolate on the stove, adding an entire bottle of cherry cough syrup for flavor.

When we sat in a circle to play Pretty Kitty, it was Mary Lou who made us laugh the most. When she got down on all fours, smiled, looked deeply into our eyes, and meowed, it was impossible to look at her round, pimply face, and pet her greasy hair without laughing. Elaine said the game was silly and refused to play. Her sister went to her room and slammed the door behind her.

For Hot and Cold, we clapped loud and fast when Carolyn, blindfolded, got near enough to touch a prized bag of M&Ms. When it was Susan's turn, she tripped and fell over the dining table, where the bag was in the center. When she started to cry, Elaine shouted, "Transport the injured!" Jenny and I clasped our hands to make a seat and then carried Susan, her legs sticking straight out, to and around the living room, up a step to the dining room, around the dining table, and back again where she kicked up a leaf of the tea table holding a stack of perfectly aligned *LIFE* and *LOOK* magazines. When Elaine yelled, "Watch where you're going!" we stopped and stood Susan back up onto her feet.

Elaine went and brought three of her father's neckties for us to use as blindfolds, and we paired off: Elaine and Jenny, Mary Lou and Susan, and Carolyn and me. We played the hard version of Blindfold, allowing only our ring fingers to touch each other as a guide for one girl to lead the other blindfolded girl around. We kept bumping into one another and laughing. After a while we collapsed into giggles.

There weren't really enough of us to play Gossip, so the message that "Carolyn's mother is pregnant" whispered into the first girl's ear was still "Carolyn's mother is pregnant" by the end of the line.

The next game was Trust, which I hated. Everyone watched as one of us girls fell backward into the arms of another girl. Jenny was supposed to catch me, but I turned to my side and caught myself with my arms. I was what my Granny called a worrier.

"Chicken! You lose," Elaine proclaimed.

"Oh, ye of little faith," Carolyn said.

I felt bad in addition to scared. We'd learned to play Trust in the basement of our church at our Sunday night youth group of which Carolyn was vice president. But even in the church, I couldn't let myself fall backward into possible nothingness or trust someone who might be temporarily distracted. I had to look after my own life and skull.

"Let's dance now," Elaine said, walking over to her case of record albums.

"Not yet," Elaine's sister had come out of her bedroom. She stood in front of us with a solemn expression and held a red candle in a Christmas star-shaped holder. "You have to summon the ghost of Bloody Mary to join you here" she said, carrying a book of matches that she used to light the candle. "Follow me," she said, leading us down the hall to the bathroom where we crowded inside.

Placing the candle next to the sink, she told us, "Now, find your face in the mirror. Get where you can see. You have to slowly chant 'Bloo–dy Mar–y' thirteen times, with your eyes closed. You'll see her. If you peek, she can scar your face . . . and put claw marks all over your body."

"She gave her mother forty whacks with an axe," Susan said.

"No," Mary Lou said. "This is the Mary who put Protestants on a stick if they wouldn't turn Catholic. Burned some, too. And cut off their heads."

"That's disgusting!" we said, but the details made us apprehensive. Elaine's sister turned off the light.

"This is lame," Carolyn said. "Do we have to do this?"

"Yes, we do now," Elaine's sister said, "because we've said her name. Close your eyes tight."

The chanting began, hurried until we were seized by the possibility of ghosts. We slowed down our repetitions of "Bloo–dy, Mar–y." The light flashed on and off three times.

"Look for her," Elaine's sister said.

Those in the back of the bathroom screamed. They said they'd seen a flash of red blood. I saw red dots under my eyelids. When Carolyn looked in the mirror, she said that her face was mashed flat like a pink pancake with ketchup. Jenny said that her face had scratch marks that hadn't been there before.

"Let me out of here!" I yelled. My hair looked to me as if it were blazing with hundreds of scarlet fireflies. The candle had mysteriously gone out. "Let's go dance."

"Yes," Elaine said. "I've got 'Sincerely' and 'Love Is a Many Splendored Thing.'"

Jenny and Carolyn squealed with delight.

Elaine's sister said she only danced with boys, and then she trooped back down the hallway toward her room.

We followed Elaine to the den, where she set up the record player and the 45s. At first, we emulated the dance steps from *American Bandstand*. We shook our elbows and rocked our knees to "Rock Around the Clock." We began to perspire. Susan took off her sweater and skirt and danced in her undershirt, half-slip, and panties. Her underwear was real and adult—pastel with lace and not made by Carters. It could have been Maidenform or Vanity Fair. Elaine took off her undershirt and then disappeared for a few minutes. She returned carrying beautiful black and white satin slips from her mother's chest of drawers. We stripped off our tops and put on the slips that smelled like cedar and roses. We glowed. We swayed and sang to "Mr. Sandman."

Then Elaine showed us her father's brand-new stereo in the living room. She opened his leather box full of vinyl albums of classical music, including *Moonlight Sonata, Sonata Pathetique, Boléro, Scherazade*, and the *Wedding March*. Jenny said that she'd seen belly dancers in *National Geographic*, so she showed us how to move our stomachs in and out while spinning slowly in a circle.

"I am a woman of mystery," Susan said, draping her face with an extra slip by hanging it over her ears.

Wanting to cover my face without losing the moment, because a pause would stop the earth from turning, I grabbed the corner of the nearest window's casement curtain, stuffed it into my mouth, and wrapped my 96-pound body in its sheerness. Arms above my head as I twirled, I felt as weightless as voile. More than anything, I wanted to be a ballerina like Anna Pavlova or Maria Tallchief, in spite of the fact that my ballet and tap dance teacher had informed me that "You can't get there from here, honey."

I tried spinning into thirty-two pirouettes. As I spun, I heard applause from the other girls—Jenny, Carolyn, Susan, Mary Lou, and even Elaine. I spiraled out into the living room and then back toward the window. My friends each grabbed a sheer curtain too. As "Boléro" played, our bodies swayed to the left and right and the curtains spread out like wings. There were six white casement curtains under the matching brocade cornices of the three windows—enough for us to do the Dance of the Six Veils. We were Arabian princesses, each with the weight of a curtain's corner between our lips. Mary Lou had wound herself into a cocoon. She was an encased Madonna, almost beautiful. We were Indian maidens circling a teepee, young Eskimo women sliding down a snowbank, daughters of Israel entering the Holy of Holies to see if we would be vaporized. We were May Day virgins as we circled Mrs. Bauman's tall brass floor lamp in front of the windows. We raised our arms up toward the ceiling, our sky, and then curtsied, twisting the curtains as we went. A thin ripping sound was audible. Susan stumbled over the cord that ran from the lamp to the wall. The lamp fell over, but Jenny rolled it out of our space. We were lovely brides without anyone to give us away, but together, white drapes across our shoulders, we proceeded from the window and down the "aisle" to the accompaniment of Mendelssohn's grand "Wedding March."

Suddenly, haze was in the air and manna was on our hair. It was as if the roof had collapsed and opened to the heavens, radiation falling on our graceful arms and shoulders. A loud crack shook the room as the plaster gave way and the cornices fell. The doorbell rang, plaster powder fell on the carpet, and the doorbell rang again. There was no time to move the brocade cornices off the floor. There was no time to fix the curtain rods dangling in an X shape across the picture window, like some vandalized, boarded-up pawnshop downtown. Neither time nor words could undo the damage or prevent our shame. But neither could they lessen our utter delight with our total loveliness.

Elaine dropped her curtain and ran up to her parents, who gazed at their once-perfect living room. She looked appalled. Her sister came out of her room and feigned surprise.

Almost immediately, our parents arrived. They stuffed their bad girls into a Hudson Hornet, Chevrolet Bel Air, Chrysler Town & Country station wagon, and my stepfather's Nash Rambler, like limp kudzu vines. The Presbyterian parents offered money to the Baumans to pay for the damage, but they refused. The Methodists offered to help with repairs and mow the lawn when spring came. My stepfather said they most likely would report it to their insurance company as being the result of an accident or an act of God—gravity rather than depravity.

Mr. and Mrs. Bauman transferred Elaine to a private school on the northeast side of Atlanta. The one and only time that I ever talked to Mary Lou on the phone, she told me in a whisper that she'd had to confess to a priest and say some Hail Marys using her rosary beads and that had been the end of it.

My stepfather beat me with his belt. My mother cried. They said nothing. For six months, I knew not to ask them if I could do anything outside school or church. And until I was twenty-one, I dealt with any wiggly impulses to behave foolishly by biting down on them, mashing them with my tongue, and swallowing them.

Whenever my parents said, "Not a good idea," I recalled the sinful deed in Elaine Bauman's living room. Jenny, Carolyn, Susan, and I never spoke about having lost Elaine as our friend or about that night, the one time that we had crossed over and felt the full range of our possibilities and our infinite beauty.

Under the Bell Curve

One Sunday as I was leaning against the wall in the church fellowship hall, wishing my mother would hurry up and take me home, Miss Knight, my high school Latin teacher, within earshot, said to my mother and to Mary Lou's and Valerie's, that a girl in the church had scored the highest IQ ever recorded at Southside High. Not one of the mothers asked Miss Knight the girl's name, for to do so was as forbidden as asking after someone's salary or another woman's specific female problem.

Miss Knight's piece of I.Q. information gnawed at the edges of all my thoughts. The more I decided it didn't matter, the more it did. I knew that educators complimented kids to boost their confidence and spur them on, no matter what the teacher or administrator actually thought. Sometimes I could not remember things from one day to the next, so I always put studying for tests off until the night before. Multiple choice answers were easy because I could picture a page in my textbook and read what was under the pictures. Sometimes though, my mind seized shut while I was thinking about bounded and infinite derivative curves.

That everyone in the United States could be ranked on the Stanford-Binet scale of Intelligence was a thrilling possibility to me because on the same IQ test, we could all be one nation and not divided between north and south. When graphed out, intelligent quotients made a bell curve like an upside-down tulip. In the center were half of all people, with an average score of 100.

Down one slope of the bell were the lowest scores usually made by "poor White trash" and Black kids who were fixing to drop out of school. Down the other slope were people like Benjamin Franklin, who could write, invent, and negotiate better than any of the Founding Fathers. Or Melvil Dewey who devised the Dewey Decimal System to catalogue all the books in the world; and Booker T. Washington, the author, orator, adviser to many Presidents, and founder of the Tuskegee Normal School for Colored Youth. I read his biography, studied the sepia images of him that rendered his skin golden brown, and wrote down that he said, "I will permit no man to narrow and degrade my soul by making me hate him."

There were also people on the stupid side of the curve with book learning but no common sense. If your mother is all dressed up for her birthday and asks your father, "How do I look?" he is plain dumb if he asks if she has gained weight. If you are the young Attorney General of the United States from Massachusetts, it is not smart to fly down to Alabama or Mississippi, rush in, plop your kidskin briefcase down on the Governor's desk to tell him what's what, without first asking about his family, comment on the beauty of the Capitol architecture, and the glory of the blooming azaleas and dogwoods up the sidewalk.

People liked to use that bell shape for everything. For instance, in school most of the students were C averaged and therefore clumped in the center of the curve. Then some expert decided that there should be as many A's for Excellent and B's for Above Average as there were D's for Below Average and F's for Poor. The family of everyone I knew who ever got an F was also poor. They were always moving for cheaper rent in dilapidated cars that never quite made it to its destination. In high school, our Accelerated classes were set up by the Henry Ford Foundation, which was trying to improve education for us. We were graded

A1, A2, and A3 so that we parsed out making A's into Excellent and Stupendous, Great, and only Wonderful. If you earned too many B's or any C, you had to go back into classes with regular students who took typing and Good Citizenship.

The IQ files and all grades were in the office of the high school counselor, on whom I had a big crush. After debate practice, he drove me home in his Morris Minor because I made him laugh with my sarcastic remarks and mimicry of various teachers. He talked to me like a regular person. Some afternoons I had to wait while he had appointments with other students' parents. Occasionally, he would stroll outside his office into the hall with them and I would pick up his briefcase, straighten up his desk, turn out the light, and wait at the front door.

I saw where the individual files on students were kept. Like the Wise Men doggedly following a star when they could not know where it would lead, I was full of wonder about my IQ.

Finally, one afternoon he didn't come back for his things but shouted for me to lock the door and meet him in the parking lot. Not knowing for sure what I was going to do before I did it, I made sure the door was not locked but carefully closed.

Once home, I wrote my mother a note for her to find when she came home from work saying I had left an important book at school and had gone back to retrieve it. Because I could not balance on a bicycle once I looked at the ground moving, I walked the two and a half miles to the school. There, the cleanup crew was on the second floor, the faculty parking lot, empty.

The counseling office was still unlocked. I even dared to turn on the light. Under the H's I found my file. Inside were letters from some of my teachers, which I didn't have time to read, and a photograph of the elaborate popsicle stick house I had made in art class. The IQ report box read 126 or 162. That was all I needed to know; that this test, used throughout the US, says that I am smart. My teachers and parents always tell me that I am a smart, good girl, as if hoping I will be, but at that moment I was, even though some days I forget facts, and some days I am confused by an assignment. I believed I was above average, yet it seemed that my intelligence was fickle and fleeting. I went to my locker to get a book I didn't need in case anyone had seen me come down the hall.

That night I awoke at three with a jolt.

Mrs. Knight had said that *one* of us in the church had the highest IQ, yet I had risked capture and suspension but had only checked *mine*. I would never know which one of us it was.

Monster:
after the March on Washington

I kept three flashlights concealed beneath my pillow. Straining against the hum of the night, I listened for strange sounds and watched for headlight beams pulling into our driveway. On the city bus, Black women began shoving against me slightly as they moved down the aisle to the back. Men who once looked away, now looked me in the eye, glaring. I feared that the Boogeyman who hid under beds, in closets, and behind doors might be real. Day and night, I was always afraid and jumpy of this unknown thing. It seemed to me that the adults had created a monster and now we were all afraid of it.

This excerpt is from "Being White in Atlanta during Desegregation," in *What Does It Mean to Be White in America? Breaking the White Code of Silence: A Collection of Personal Narratives,* ed. Gabrielle David and Sean Frederick Forbes, 2Leaf Press, 2016. University of Chicago Press.

When the Roll Is Called up Yonder

On the evening I killed my grandfather, we were already in our blue Nash Rambler, my sister and I in the back seat, when Grandpa came to the side window, *tap, tap, tapping, tap, tap, tapping.* After a long day that began with church, and the visit down the red clay and gravel road that lasted into the evening, I was sleepy. *Tap, tap, tapping, tap, tap.* My head was already leaning against the door, so when I felt his presence outside, I blinked, but did not look up, pretending not to see him. Still, he kept knocking on the glass. *Tap, tap, tap, tap, tapping.* Something suddenly rose up inside of me like a whooping bird cawing "Never more."

~

On Sundays, my family always went to Little Granny and Grandpa's in Clayton, Georgia. Grandpa would sit on the front porch in a tall black rocking chair, singing, humming, whistling, or mumbling to himself, while Little Granny, it seemed to me, did all the work of sweeping the porch, frying and baking in the kitchen, weeding around vegetables in the yard, bringing in eggs from the chicken coup, milking the cow and goats, and churning butter.

"*When all of life is over,*" Grandpa would sing from his rocker, "*and the work on earth is done, when the roll is called up yonder,*

I'll be there." His work had been done many years ago before he fell down a well and cracked his head.

After lunch, Little Granny would load down all the relatives, as well as strangers, with plates of leftovers, cornbread, and preserves of figs and peaches. My family would be the last to leave.

"Be a good girl for your mama," he mumbled behind the window. "You better be ready, mockingbird. Don't be caught napping at the great roll call."

"Young lady," Mama shouted from the front seat, "you lower that window." Reluctantly, I turned the handle round and round until Grandpa's pointed chin, scruffy as a briar patch, could poke through.

"The trumpet of the Lord shall sound," Grandpa bellowed into the backseat. Without his dentures, his eyes bulged above sunken cheeks, and his lips glistened with tobacco juice. *"And time shall be no more.* And He shalt rain down His wrath."

People thought Grandpa was a holy man because he could recite long passages from the Book of Revelation and short phrases from old sermons. He would moan out parts of old gospel hymns. I wondered if Grandpa was like John the Revelator, who was exiled to an island after being plunged into boiling oil that cooked his brain. They both thought Satan was personally stalking them and the rest of us, too. Grandpa thought all terrible natural events were predicted in the last book of the Bible: hurricanes, volcanoes, floods, fires, earthquakes, evil empires, a great war, and judgment upon the earth. Grandpa never forgot these terrible predictions, yet he couldn't recall his children or grandchildren's names, so he called me and my mother mockingbird, and my sister beanie.

"Now you *'Sing Hosanna, sing Hosanna,'*" he ordered, moving closer and closer until his whole head was against my face.

As his spit splattered across my lap, I started turning the handle with my left hand, slowly cranking the window all the way up, cutting off his head, his lips making a chortling sound as if the bones in the back of his neck had shattered.

Grandpa never spoke after I did that, but the family believed he could still hear, so in 1959 when I was 15 and he was too weak to stand, Mama said I had to be the one to go read the Bible to him because he loved me the most.

By then, Little Granny and Grandpa had moved from the big farmhouse into a four-room cottage my stepfather helped build for them. Grandpa was lying on an iron bedstead in a small square room with dark brown stained window mouldings and doors. The dim air hung thick with camphor and sweat. A chair was waiting for me by his bedside. A white chenille spread was tightly pulled up under his arms and his eyes stared at the ceiling.

I read him all the stories about Moses in Exodus, Moses being prohibited from entering the Promised Land after working so hard to interpret God's rules to the Israelites. I noticed that his spread was turning black around his body, and the smell grew so bad that when his two sons arrived to see him, they only touched him on the shoulder, looked in the narrow closet for his black suit and shoes, and left the room. One took Grandpa's shoes to the living room to give them a spit polish, and the other went to the kitchen to go over the list of pallbearers with Little Granny.

When they left, I decided that he could no longer understand Biblical passages so that I would sing instead. I picked the fruit salad camp song, since it had strung together all the hymns Grandpa liked anyway.

When the roll is called up yonder,
I'll be walking down the King's highway.
Tell me the old, old story.
I love it better every day.
Halleluiah.

I will make you fishers of men
If you'll only follow me.
Halleluiah, What a Savior!
I'm from sin set-
You're from sin set-
We're all from sin set free.

Grandpa's chest heaved and he threw up yellow-brown bile and mucous. Little Granny brought a dishcloth to wipe off his mouth and chest and put crushed ice on his lower lip. His oldest daughter, a nurse, came in.

"Tarry feces," she said, leaving the room to return to the porch. "It won't be long."

Grandpa's rapid breathing pushed his swollen, quivering stomach up and down. He started making a noise that sounded like a name. Jordan? Did he mean the river "Jordan's stormy banks"?

"That's his father," Little Granny said, leaning over to hear. "He died when your grandpa was eight. His mother, Martha, went when he was ten."

Suddenly, he stopped breathing, gasped, and mouthed, "Agbar" and "Elisha."

"His brother and grandfather," Granny interpreted.

I knew Mama didn't want to be there, but I hoped that she would come get me soon. Grandpa's legs thrashed and he threw up his arms, choked, and fell back on the bed.

Little Granny held down his eyelids until they stayed closed.

I gave him a benediction.

"When the roll is called up yonder, you will step forward and say, 'Here am I.'"

I wondered what would happen if the deceased was not paying attention or wandered out of the line. Nobody would go fetch anyone because it was every man for himself. My youth group's song, called "Do Lord, Oh Do Lord, Oh Do Remember Me" included everyone. One verse was, "I'll wear the long white robe and you wear the crown." Another went, "I take Jesus as my savior, you take him too. Look away beyond the blue."

Little Granny brought a basin with warm soapy water for the woman down the road who was coming to wash his private parts. Grandma wiped down his face and head, under his chin and arms, then his fingers. She softly kissed him on his broken head.

But I could not kiss a man who had died twice.

Class Reunion

Do you remember how all the horses on the merry-go-round
    faced forward, never to turn their heads back
to laugh at a child afraid to slip out of the saddle?

Do you remember how the orbs on the Ferris wheel stayed
    concentric and did not detach or fly off except once,
when the cast iron swing set in our yard fell over in the
    summer?

Do you remember that when boys swung on the ropes
of kudzu in Carved Tree Gulley, they did not fall,
chafe their legs, tear their clothes, or get caught?

Do you remember that when Jerry Jackson
blew off his face with fireworks on the Fourth
his name was never again mentioned at school?

Do you remember Mary in our school crèche,
blonde and blue-eyed with Baby Jesus,
a pock-marked wall-eyed doll missing a leg?

Do you remember that when Kay Oliver went away
for eight months to see her dear great aunt,
she did not bring home a baby, but *Forever Amber*?

Do you remember how two people won Most Likely to Succeed,
one, Most Likely to Cry, and everyone
got a plastic trophy with a smiley face?

Can you remember the fireflies in jars who died by morning
and that when we pried with sticks the shell off a turtle,
the insides looked like our flesh?

Laying the Pattern

In 1962, temporary summer government jobs were mandated for minorities, so the plans I'd made after high school graduation to type again for the Internal Revenue Service, to save money for college, fell through. My mother argued with the government all the way to Washington, D.C., claiming that I already had two summers of experience, that I could type seventy words per minute without errors, and was the smartest girl in southwest Atlanta.

"I'm sorry ma'am," the IRS representative apologized to Mama over the phone, "but meeting racial quotas is the current priority for the civil service at this time. Even if she was the highest scorer, she would not be hired."

"I don't know why Black girls and White girls can't work at the same time. Why can't we type in the same room?" I asked Mama, who said it just couldn't happen that way. "Then I could show them how I change the form letters and they might know how to fix letters to people who say they can't pay their taxes and give a good reason. How many years have Black people been excluded from working for any government agency, except as janitors?" I asked.

"That's beside the point, young lady," my stepfather responded. "Those ideas you learned from those seminary students at Camp Calvin won't buy you textbooks." They sent me out to sweep the garage and said that the light in my room had better be off an hour earlier than usual, which was 10 p.m.

The college sent me an announcement that the freshman discussion book was William Golding's *Lord of the Flies*. My grandmother, who taught me spelling and the multiplication tables, gave me her flashlight, and I hid it under my pillow so that I could read the rest of the summer reading list when I couldn't sleep. Also included in the envelope with the list was an invitation to a tea and faculty reception. I'd never been to a tea, except to the Magnolia Tea Room at Rich's Department Store where I once had Chicken Salad Amandine and their frozen fruit salad, I wondered what I should wear to a reception and tea.

Belle Henderson lay in bed, imagining what she might make special for her granddaughter to wear in September. Her eyelids were heavy and puffy in the morning, but by midday they had wrinkled and tightened so that she could fully open her eyes that she needed for the one last thing that she was determined to do.

Bonnie was going off to that college where all the fine ladies had gone for whom Belle had done tailoring and dressmaking. Bonnie was almost a grown lady, and the first granddaughter on either side of the family to be going to college. While Belle's sister, Chloe Wallace, went to teacher's college, Belle Wallace became infatuated with 17-year-old Claude Henderson. When he disappeared, and she became the head of household, she fed her two sons by working fifteen years for Scottish Rite Hospital making pajamas for children with club feet, so she knew exactly how to cut a pattern that would make her granddaughter look her best. When Bonnie had to recite the Westminster Catechism before the Elders at the Presbyterian Church, adding comments where Martin Luther would have disagreed with Calvin, Belle

Henderson had made her a pink dress with roses on the yoke to soften her words. For Bonnie's declamation speeches, Granny made a blue suit, for strength. Bonnie wore a red tailored dress, for daring, when she was awarded first Negative Speaker in debate. All the skirts were exactly 26 inches long. For the college tea she would make a pastel dress with a matching jacket.

My Latin teacher and the librarian, after I made a good score on the preliminary SAT, recommended that I go to the best girls' college in the South in Decatur, GA, which cost more than going to the University of Georgia. Finally, the State Department of Education informed me that I had been approved for a Georgia State Teacher Scholarship to teach in Georgia public schools for five years. A lot of teachers had quit because integrated classrooms might happen. When my stepfather told me I would major in Education, I said that I couldn't because I was going to be a novelist or an editor of the *Saturday Review*. My parents signed my name anyway to the State Department of Education scholarship agreement that would pay $600 an academic year.

I thought I could earn extra money and not have to promise to teach school for five years, so I answered an ad in the paper for a personal secretary. The man had a nice voice and asked me about my grade average and job experience. But then his tone changed into a whisper. He wanted to know if I had bathed feet before, which my relatives at Stone Mountain always did, so I said, "Yes." Had I ever kissed a woman's toes, stroked her feet, and licked the inside of her shoes? I put the receiver down carefully, fearing my Granny might hear. Soon after, Mama got me a job at Third Army as a Clerk Typist where I saved up $750 in the credit union.

As a clerk typist, all I had to do was fill in for file clerks who were on summer vacation. The women in my office nagged me about everything. Why didn't I buy myself a new miniskirt so I could catch the eye of some soldier? Why didn't I tweeze my eyebrows into a thinner arch? Why didn't I get my hair cut and teased into a bubble? Regardless, it was clear to me that these women did most of the work, yet none of them were above the federal pay scale of a 6. They knew the weaknesses and incompetencies of the men who were on a pay scale of 9 to 13, but instead of actively competing for higher positions, they vented their aggression by keeping track of any and all indiscretions of the officers.

My mother believed that even if she applied for a man's job, she'd never get it; instead, she would be labeled as "pushy" and eventually demoted. When a Black officer without any management experience at all was transferred in as a GS-11, two of the women quit. The bosses said it was because the women were "going through the change" and couldn't stand pressure anymore. When the other men left for lunch together, they never asked the new man to "come along with us." At the supper table, when Mama fussed about the new hire, Granny and I kept quiet, but that night after I straightened Granny's blankets, she began to pray for comfort and bravery for the GS-11 because he was alone, she said, while the women had one another.

Granny Henderson opened and closed her cramped hands, pulling on the knuckles of each finger, for in the morning, her hands were stiff, sore, and cold as if they had been caught in the crevice of a window all night. She looked at her crooked fingers, remembering when Bonnie used to paint her nails with clear polish. Now they had a gray cast, and the cuticles grew over the thick edges. Reaching for her glasses on the nightstand, she sat up and swung her legs off the bed and thought of the dress she'd make. First, she'd position the pattern on the straight grain of the material, pin it, mark the darts, and cut it out. Then she'd baste the dress together, stitch it on the sewing machine, finish all the handwork, and have it ready for Bonnie's tea. Her daughter-in-law wanted her to stay in bed all day. Everyone seemed afraid that she might fall, break her hip, and not be able to get to the telephone to ask for help. She would rather take risks than to die in bed.

To hold herself together, she put on a corset, and wore her rayon dress with the print of sombreroed Mexicans napping across the bodice to remind herself that she mustn't take a nap. She put on the Sunday lace-up black shoes that she never wore anymore because she didn't have transportation to get to the open-air tabernacle. The shoes were tight on her feet, and she couldn't lean over to tie them.

Granny Henderson pulled from under the side of the bed the box of yellow Irish linen that she'd secretly ordered from the Sears, Roebuck & Co. catalog. She was going to duplicate a fashionable sheath dress with a jacket, which had been on the front page of the Society section of the *Atlanta Journal*. The material was supposed to be the color of dandelions opening, but when it arrived the linen was pale, as if April's showers had diluted it with bleach. Bonnie would be just as beautiful in pale yellow.

The pattern pieces she had cut out were also under the bed in a flat box, next to a small one used to stash crackers and peanut butter so that she wouldn't have to go to the kitchen when she got hungry in the middle of the night. Bonnie's parents said she made too much noise "banging" her walker down the hallway. She couldn't understand how they could hear that noise but fail to respond whenever she commented on anything in the same room. The cortisone for her arthritis had made her partially deaf, but everyone else in the house, except Bonnie, seemed partially deaf, too.

She couldn't use the kitchen table for cutting out the dress because she'd surely strow scraps on the floor and wouldn't be able to stoop and pick them up. If she cut it on her bed, she'd be in real trouble if she accidentally cut the bedspread, so she took off the bedspread and dropped it on the rug. Bracing her knees against the bed, she pushed her walker to the side to smooth out the fabric and pin the pattern pieces on carefully. Her scissors were sharp because she had a rule that they could not be used on anything but fabric or thread. When her head began to swim and her eyes would no longer focus, she raised herself and grabbed onto the walker. A sprig of damp white hair kept falling across her eyes.

I waited until my mother was involved in one of her long telephone conversations to lock myself in the bathroom. I had read in *Mademoiselle* magazine about how to shape eyebrows. Laying a ruler straight up beside my nose, I made a mark with an eyebrow pencil where my eyebrows began. Then I measured along the ruler, from the edge of my nose to the outside corner of my eye and put a dot where my eyebrows should end. With my mother's tweezers, I began pulling out the hairs on either side of those marks. Then I started pulling the stray hairs under my eyebrows. As I plucked, my eyes watered, and my nose ran; it hurt.

The article said to look straight ahead and make the center of the pupil the highest point of the arch. I discovered that it didn't hurt any worse to pull three or four hairs at once. Every time I pulled some hairs on one eyebrow, I had to pull some on the other eyebrow to make them symmetrical, so I pulled some more.

"Honey," Granny started, squinting at my face, "I think you may have ruined your expression. You look like you're waiting for the answer to a question." She paused and smiled at me, "But you've always had a tendency to overdo."

"I suppose," I replied.

"Except for having children," she said, "almost anything you mess up can be fixed."

Whenever I came in from a date, after enduring my stepfather's questions, I went down the hall to Granny's bedroom and told her the who, what, and where of the evening—not for her approval or disapproval, but as if I were speaking in my own mind to hear what it was thinking. Granny was the one who raised a caution about the tall young man I met at church named Stephen Cone who carried his deceased father's brown hat, without ever putting it on, even placing it in the center of the table when we went out to eat. Granny said to tell him I was sick.

As I talked, I would let the loose braid fall against her back and brush out her hair. Streaked with gray and yellow, it had been growing since the day she was born.

One evening I locked the bathroom door, found my mother's box of tampons, and read the instructions. I propped my leg up on the toilet seat and tried to assume the position from the picture. I pushed and pushed the cotton tube in different places, but it wouldn't go in. I found a mirror and used it to try to find my hole. My legs trembled. The inside of me was purplish red and ugly.

Friday morning, Granny Henderson was feeling so energetic that she decided to wash her hair with Ivory soap and rinse it with lemon juice. She went into the kitchen to do it, deciding she would come back later and wipe up the water on the counter and floor if it didn't dry on its own. Wrapping a turquoise towel around her shoulders, she went down the steps to the breezeway and outside to dry her hair. Bonnie's parents would be aghast if they knew she was outside. When she was a child in Stone Mountain, GA, the front yard of a house had been for waiting for a baby to be born, washing visitor's feet, drying your hair, feeding children lunch, telling stories, making contracts with a handshake, and basting and hand stitching on quilt pieces when the sun was so bright that it made your needles glisten. But since the neighborhood had integrated, no one used the front yards anymore. As she went back inside, she turned to look over her shoulder and thought she glimpsed her baby daughter Wilma who died in the flu epidemic of 1918. She picked a dandelion near her ankle, blew its skeletal fuzz into the air, and stuck the stem in her pocket.

On Monday, Granny Henderson sat down at the sewing machine and stitched up the basted bust darts and seams of the yellow dress using two bobbins that she'd hand-wound in the middle of the night. Not once did her hands vary the width of the seams. Not once did the fine thread slip out of the machine's needle. She pressed the seams open against the edges of the cabinet. The basting thread slipped out of the seams without leaving a wrinkle.

At the end of the summer, a nice woman at work me gave me a bottle of TABU.

"Dab it on the pulse points on the insides of your wrists and behind your knees," she instructed me, indicating those areas on her own body. "As your body perspires, the fragrance rises."

I could put the perfume on when I went to Carly Hart's toga party. She had invited everyone from our Latin class. Taking off my clothes, I grabbed a sheet from the linen closet and tried to drape it over one shoulder and securely under the other arm. My arms looked fat. Or maybe they didn't if I kept them out. My neck was too long, and I needed stockings because my legs weren't tan. I couldn't wear sandals because I had long ugly toes. Who wanted to go to a dumb toga party anyway?

Granny Henderson needed some tiny pearl buttons for the back neck of the dress, and she still needed a lining for the jacket. From the hall closet, she pulled out two boxes of scraps from all the dresses she'd made, but nothing was suitable. The only silky fabric she could think of was the oyster-colored lining of her own camel coat. She supposed she'd never need it again to go to town or hear Miss Barth's preaching at the tabernacle. Bonnie's mother didn't approve of speaking in tongues in public. Granny pulled out the coat, laid it over her walker, hauled it to her bedroom, and cut out the lining. For the buttons, she thought of the dresses she'd made for Bonnie's Toni doll. What had happened to those? Then she thought of the black crepe dress with a white crocheted collar and tiny white pearl buttons she was saving for her burial. She found it in a zippered bag and cut off the buttons. The mortician could pull the sides of her collar together, or she could replace them when she had time.

~

I was trying to write a paper about *Lord of the Flies*. It seemed to me that the group of boys on the island was a microcosm of human history. Someone tries to take over by inventing an enemy; anyone different becomes the scapegoat. Together, even boys who could have thought for themselves, when they became part of a tribe, were willing to do horrible things like a pack of wolves. I wondered whether girls left alone to set up their own society might construct it differently or would they invent popular clubs for the popular ones?

~

Through the window next to her bed, Granny Henderson watched the five-o'clock traffic, which was hectic and restless as if the drivers were chasing the sun that moved down steadily ahead of them. Their speed made her aware that she'd done nothing with Bonnie's dress for the past week. Bonnie and her mother were on their way home from shopping for shoes, so she needed to be in bed. She pulled the sheet up to her neck. Her daughter-in-law had taken the bedspread off saying that Granny must have had a small stroke getting out of bed and dropped the bedspread. She was afraid next that Granny might lose control of her bladder and then her mind. The pale-yellow dress was neatly rolled in a box under her bed. She knew she should show it to Bonnie's mother for approval, but in the backyard of her mind, she knew that any seeming collaboration with her mother would make the gift unacceptable to Bonnie.

Tomorrow she would tack the lining of the jacket in position: center back, center shoulder, and front darts. She imagined the dress on a mannequin at the foot of her bed, the stitches as tiny and even as those on Bonnie's christening dress, the bodice the length of her fourth-grade hand-knit sweaters, the skirt the exact length as her pleated speech making skirts. A truck passed by on the street, and the bars of the blinds trembled. The arms and thighs of the mannequin appeared to bust out of the dress. When Bonnie knocked on Granny Henderson's bedroom door, bringing supper on a tray, she said she didn't feel like eating.

I knew my grandmother was up to something, but I didn't know what. Occasionally, in the middle of the night, I heard her humming. But when I tiptoed down to her room and peeked inside, she was sleeping.

"She's turning senile," my mother said. "She doesn't know what she's doing anymore. I found the string and wrappings of a tampon in one of her pockets. You need to start pressing your own clothes yourself. We can't trust your grandmother with the iron anymore."

Granny Henderson started on the dress' zipper, putting it in by hand on the wrong side and then catching single threads of the fabric on the top side. She ripped the hem tape off her summer robe and stitched it to the bottom edge of the dress. When it was finished, she hung it on a hanger over the top drawer of her dresser. How long ago had it been that she and her cousins and sister Chloe hung their dresses on Saturdays nights, with a fresh flower on the collar? Her daughter-in-law said that Bonnie had gone to a movie with her boyfriend, Alan. Turning off the overhead light, Granny waited for Bonnie to come home and brush out her hair. Then she'd surprise her with the pale-yellow dress.

Past ten, she was still waiting. She wasn't tired. She was propped up in bed. A breeze from the window swept across the room, lifting the hem of the yellow dress. She felt calm, very still, just waiting, perhaps—she didn't know—dreaming. If she lived until Bonnie graduated from college and married, maybe she'd go to live with them. Since Bonnie didn't know how to cook anything except scrambled eggs and brownies, she could cook for them like she used to do for a Greek family. Bonnie's mother never allowed anyone near the pressure cooker, which she had to use when she got home from work to get supper on the table fast. On Sundays they went to lunch in the country.

⤙

I kissed Alan goodnight under the gas lamp at the edge of the driveway instead of at the front door, which my stepfather usually opened as soon as he heard footsteps. For no particular reason, I always lied when I answered his questions, but he never knew the difference. He looked at my clothes and commented if they were wrinkled. If I forgot to reapply it, he and Mama pointed out that my lipstick had worn off. Then he would turn off the lights in the living room and send me to bed.

Was it too late to go see Granny? When I walked quietly to her room, she was sitting up in bed. I turned on her overhead light, but she didn't look up. Picking up her hairbrush from the dresser, I walked to her bedside and took the pins out of her bun.

Her head fell forward, and I leaned it back against the pillow. Her hands were in her lap, palms up, holding her red felt pincushion that was stuffed with my childhood hair. At the end of her bed, hanging on an open drawer, was a tailored, pale yellow dress with matching jacket. I looked at the invisible hem. It was too long to be for my short mother. It had to be for me. My Granny loved me. She loved me whether I was dumb or smart, whether I was awkward or poised. I carried the dress to my room, hung it carefully in my closet, and went to bed. The next morning, I told my mother to check on Granny because she might have had a stroke.

By the day of the college tea, most of Granny's things had been packed up to go to a nursing home. When I returned home, I went back to her room. I told her that several people had complimented my dress. I told her that many of the girls had worn black dresses in August, and that each of them seemed to have a strand of pearls. I didn't actually meet anyone except some faculty members, who were very cordial and asked me what I had read recently. They were dressed quite plainly in tailored suits made from dull worsted or gabardine.

I enjoyed listening to conversations. Many of the other girls knew how to gracefully walk around the room and talk to strangers. I described to Granny all the details of the furniture, the tea service, and the colors in the antique carpet. Although she could no longer comment, I knew she heard me as she always had and always would. As soon as I'd mastered listening, she began to comfort me and encourage me, patting my hands and whispering softly in tongues

Walking on Water

I never liked thin, saltless grits with a pat of bright yellow margarine melting in the center, and I liked even less my mother cooling it by adding water, which only made more of the stuff. How old would I have to be to say what I wanted and didn't want to eat? Would the sky fall if I didn't eat something to "stick to yer ribs" before I caught the 6:45 bus in front of my home to classes across town? Why couldn't I eat downtown on my own money when I changed buses? The Krystal's square burgers with ground beef and steamed in onions were only twelve cents. Why couldn't I eat in the dining hall with the other girls when I arrived at school? Because my mama couldn't then be certain that I had done it.

I was later and later coming to the breakfast table because selecting what I was going to wear out of the clothes my mother had purchased seemed the only choice I was allowed to make. The areas of study at college were fixed: English Literature, New Testament, Classics, Botany, and French. Weeknights I couldn't choose to stay up late to read because my stepfather threw the circuit to my bedroom and the attic at 10 o'clock.

The only way to avoid going to church on Sunday was to say I had cramps about which my stepfather would never question me. I hated church because adults told me to enjoy my fun life while I could. They asked me what I was studying and what I wanted to be, and I was expected to say "teacher" and "mother." The preacher said absolutely nothing to someone who was exhausted, alienated, sad, and angry, a human oxymoron, or a plain moron.

As a day student, I actually liked riding the bus to school because I loved to people-watch and also because passengers left newspapers on the seats. The Israelis hung Adolf Eichmann, chief organizer of the Final Solution. He claimed that he had no choice in planning the transportation and design of gas chambers to murder millions because he was being obedient to his superiors. When we learned that the USSR had 39 atomic reactors, our government decided to build 200. We didn't get to vote on that. One hundred thousand babies whose mothers agreed to take Thalidomide for morning sickness had been born with stunted and missing limbs or died. Prayer was banned in public schools, which was a good thing, since it was used on the morning intercom to ask the good Lord to bless the football team but not to protect James Meredith entering the University of Mississippi. Why didn't the minister of my church ever preach about any of these events from his pulpit?

I decided to make my own study room in the attic by moving my books up the steep steps and piling up the family luggage and boxes of dead relatives' clothes that mama always kept. Did she think they were coming back for them? I spread out the books I had to hide downstairs because they weren't assigned reading: the poet laureates of Mississippi, mystic prayers, a Sanskrit dictionary, Renaissance drawings of the humours. I took my Underwood typewriter and one poster of John Glenn, astronaut. I spread quilts on the floor, but I was not allowed to sleep up there lest I "catch pneumonia." Mama tried to entice me back to my room by bringing in a rose brocaded chair from the living room and buying a lavender lamp for reading with china violets around the top of the shade. I told her that Virginia Woolf said I should have a "room of one's own." She said I was ungrateful for what my parents provided through a lot of sacrifice, that I was headstrong and unthoughtful. That was true.

Because I was not making all A's, and even a D in French, Mr. Merritt continually charged up the stairs to my attic space to find out if I was doing the assignments. Without thinking or blinking I could make up hypothetical projects.

"Two professors have assigned term papers," I told him. "With materials that cannot be checked out from the library."

Looking for the lie, he watched me from the top of the attic staircase.

"I'll have to stay late at school," I told him.

I loved the over-sized smooth oak reading tables and brass reading lamps in the college library. To make my lying truthful, I started reading uncirculated literary magazines. Then I wandered up and down aisles, reaching for the wedged book on top shelves that had never been checked out. I sought the lonely, overlooked volumes, looking for connections; the unexpected tie with the neighboring book, continually circling all the eccentric unappreciated minds in the search for someone, anyone promising, but peculiar, angry, longing. Someone like me.

When the library lights blinked at quarter to ten, I asked an upperclassman on the steps when Blackfriars was staging *Waiting for Godot,* and consequently did not catch the bus until eleven. My mind was so full of new phrases that I rested my tired head against a window where the rhythmic bumping of my temple against the cold glass was comforting.

I forgot to pull on the cord that alerted the driver to stop, so I had to yell to the front. Black people would push open the rear door and jump off without raising their voice to get the driver's attention. Sometimes I didn't know if the minute before I had rung the bell, so I would pull on the cord again, an action that usually made the driver angry, so that he would pull away from the curb, abruptly causing me to drop my papers and books. I waited at my stop to get on the bus headed to southwest Atlanta. Because I was there, the bus would stop for the Black maids waiting, instead of speeding by.

The transfer stop was across from The Three Sisters, an economical women's apparel shop. On the third floor, a glass box displayed three mannequins with thin, out-of-date plaster that looked like wrinkled skin. Their arms, with fingers tilted up, were fixed at an angle to lightly brush the sides of a taffeta ball gown. Sometimes, one of them would be missing her wig. In miniskirts above their hinged, dimpled pink knees, fingers still tilted up, they looked ridiculous, these aliens looking down on Atlanta.

Day after day there had been rain and thunder, mud on hubcaps and grills, wet clothes, and soggy papers, yet in the bus seats up front sat White second shift waitresses or hospital nursing assistants with soiled smocks who lacked raincoats. Black maids made to stay late to set up for a dinner party, leaving their own children alone at home, sunk with a sigh on the torn vinyl back seats. A few derelicts called "bums" slept in their seats, staying on as long as the driver would let them. A withered man in faded blue overalls beneath a Civil War vintage dress coat, reached out to grab the pole next to my seat but fell backwards against another rider.

"Don't you touch me," the bald-headed rider yelled. "Get away!"

I got up, gave the man my seat, and moved toward the back where a white-headed older Black man and a little boy occupied the rear bench seat. The boy leaned his head against the old man's shoulder, who I thought might be his grandfather, but the man pushed the little boy away. Then, the boy turned his back to the man and tried to lay his small head in the old man's lap but, again, the man pushed him away. The boy began to whimper, but I was unable to get up out of my seat and make a move to comfort him, to smile or wiggle my fingers in my ears to distract him.

I wondered if anyone in a circle of White girls in our organdy dresses, gathered smiling around the church piano, would cuddle this child in clothes that didn't come from Rich's Department Store? My legs wouldn't move from my seat.

Our parents all beamed when we sang in church. The tune to "Jesus Loves the Little Children" was catchy because it was the same tune as "Tramp, Tramp, Tramp, the Boys are Marching" for Civil War soldiers.

"Jesus loves the little children,
all the children of the world.
Red and yellow, black and white,
they are precious in his sight.
Jesus loves the little children of the world."

Jesus might love them. We didn't know them, so we could not love them.

The little boy laid down on the green seat and cautiously edged his feet into his elder's lap.

"I'm gonna cut off dem toes," said the old man.

I imagined the boy wiggling his toes in his sock feet across my lap.

"Oh, forget it," the old man gave in, flicking his wrinkled fingers. "Put your feet up here."

As the rain began to fall deliberately, sliding long finger marks down the bus windows, the driver leaned forward to see across his wipers. I had on my taupe trench coat, the one thing I had begged for at Christmas because my English professor wore one. My stop was near, so I gathered my books and purse and headed for the back door. I paused on the wet bottom step. The doors opened and I looked down into a torrent of rainwater rushing against the curb. Was there a dead pigeon in it? A black raven? Somebody's faded turquoise quilted house shoe? I would surely slip in the water and be drug under the bus and run over. My Granny said to be careful and not to slip in the tub. Didn't the doctor say when I couldn't urinate that I should sit in the warm water for an hour, but he didn't look at me as he said it. I couldn't move from the step.

"Are you getting off or aren't you?" yelled the bus driver

"Wrong stop," I muttered and returned to my seat.

Now what? Get off at the next stop? I couldn't. Ride to the end of the line and back again? Lightning split the sky outside and cracked against the membrane in my ears. The boy on the back seat sat up and began to cry while the old man snored. At the periphery of my vision, daggers of light punctured the horizon. Then rain fell so fast that it obliterated seeing. My mother would be fussing because I didn't take my umbrella or my galoshes. My stepfather would be checking the phones to make sure I could get through if I called. They did not deserve to be worried about me. Why was I always causing them anxiety? Why did I feel responsible for their happiness? Accused. Accursed.

Now I was in an unfamiliar section of town and could not transfer to the right bus. *The beginning and principle of all things is water.* That was Thales the Milesian. Why couldn't I remember that on my exam? Did my fingers look wrinkled? Did God wait, as Genesis said, to create humans until after He made light and finished moving over the water. Water, water, everywhere.

I bit my arm, like I bit the pillows in my closet when I was eight, and sucked the blood.

"There will be no guests at your wedding because you are so unfriendly, so clumsy," the Ancient Mariner folded back my ear with his skinny hand and whispered, "You will disappoint your parents by flunking out of school. Have you noticed that you mix up the facts? You can't even construct an outline until after you've written the essay. You can't drive a car or steer a bike. You can't memorize a sonata or an ode. You scream at your mother. You should be ashamed." He whispered on and on.

The child on the back seat sobbed, hugging his own head at each clap of thunder, interrupting the voices from my brain.

"Go away," I said. "You raise phlegm in my throat."

The old man opened his bleary eyes and looked out.

"Jesus, Lord," he exclaimed.

Jesus could walk on water, but I would sink like Simon Peter, distracted by looking at the coming gale about to destroy his boat for I am always getting distracted. Strangers threw Jonah overboard to quiet the storm they blamed on him, but he survived being swallowed by the great fish because he finally obeyed. I didn't want to obey. Get me home, Jesus, and I'll be good to everyone. The bargain at the end of the rainbow.

At the bow of the bus, water overflowed down the windshield and trickled down the edge of the inside dashboard. The bus skidded through a deep puddle and water came in over the bottom steps.

"Damn," complained the driver. "This ain't no God damned ark. I'm gwineter pull over."

The ninth descendant of Adam was derided by his neighbors for the monstrosity in his yard. Then he and all his family were imprisoned on that ark he built and covered with pitch. Noah waited forty days and Noah survived. I would survive, too. I could wait. I was patient. But one thing was certain. I wouldn't have gotten on Noah's ark in the first place, and I would not bow to a God who would destroy those who weren't invited.

Madness, Digital Collage from author's photos.
By Elizabeth Shepley, 2022.

Infirmed

The entrance to my college was a circular drive surrounded by huge Magnolia trees, but that was the only resemblance to a Southern girl's finishing school. Graduates were expected to assume leadership positions in further academic work, in journalism, in nonprofit management, and church education programs for children and adults.

"You are not parlor flowers," they said.

Although I was a day student, I had paid for a lunch ticket at the Evans dining hall. With high clerestory windows, the dining hall did not offer hamburgers or condone reading at the table. The cooks liked rhubarb, which I had never seen, and the turnip greens were chopped up in small pieces without fatback. There was neither buttermilk nor cornbread.

I shared a table in the day student lounge with Anna, a senior English major, who lived with her mother in downtown Decatur. They traveled to Europe and had season tickets to the opera and they both had psychotherapists. I was fascinated by Anna's interest in and knowledge about her mother's peculiar habits and fears based on how women in her family were raised over three generations.

Once a week, freshmen had appointments with our advisers to discuss our progress. Every week Dr. Pondergast, who was also my freshman literature and composition teacher, wanted to know if I was happy at school, a question I never considered. "Happy" was not a goal I had ever heard of. Mostly I was tired because I was not allowed to sleep late on Saturday or Sunday at home. If I put the covers over my head and didn't turn on any lights, my stepfather would still grab my foot and yank me out of bed.

"Get up and get dressed," he'd command. "You're going to church."

After the boring worship service that never mentioned the unrest in the South and our nation over desegregation, I was welcomed by adults downstairs during fellowship time. The father of a friend always came toward me with a big grin proclaiming, "If I knew you were coming, I'd have baked a cake." Other adults acknowledged that I must be working hard at such a prestigious college, that I would surely be somebody when I graduated, that my parents must be real proud of me. And many would say, "Now if you ever need anything, you just call me, you hear?"

Gordon Street Presbyterian Church was full of good people, but they thought that since the Bible didn't specifically say that slavery was a sin, that it wasn't. The national church, overseen at every level by assemblies of elder men, thought a belief in the Lord Jesus Christ as a personal savior was far more important than how we treat others. I didn't know how to speak up with my opinions except to spout off in the car going home. My stepfather, who was also an elder in the church, said that some northern ministers were drifting into liberalism and communism.

One Monday, Dr. Pondergast gave me a copy of Simone Weil's *Waiting for God,* saying that she believed knowing the author would be meaningful to me. When I read the short book, I learned that Weil decided to remain outside the church in order to be intellectually and artistically honest.

To me, Dr. Pondergast was striking in her tweed suits, without makeup or a husband. The Bible said that only a woman who fears the Lord was to be praised and never for her outward appearance. I doubted that Dr. Pondergast feared the Lord or any man. When she grasped the sides of her tabletop lectern and lifted up a word or phrase from Old English through the tongues of Chaucer and British and Irish poets, I felt elation and awe. She could speak from inside the author's mind from one word to the inevitable next, causing the very last word to breathe.

Students sat on the floor outside her door awaiting their names called from her rasping throat. She smoked unfiltered Pall Malls. For all the red marks of mistakes and questions on my papers that scalloped the edges, I hung on to each comment: *You are on to something. Better than the last. Clear but suggestive at same time. Brilliant, but do you know why?*

I began to look up words in the 20 volumes of the *Oxford English Dictionary*. Dr. Pondergast went to Oxford University and her academic robe with black torn fabric tatters at the hem was older than she was. Other girls taking down the heavy volumes of the OED never asked me what word I was curious about, yet they talked to each other. Was I becoming invisible like pure spirit? Was I like Simone Weil – "the color of dead leaves, like certain unnoticed insects?" Why did I know what it was like to be a butterfly pinned live into an album? Why did I get a stomachache if I stared at a girl reading distressing news from home? Why did my heart hurt, literally ache like a bundle of fibers being crushed in my chest? How could I understand the mysteries of literature and not understand what was happening to me?

I went to the Hub where someone was always banging out "Heart and Soul" on the piano. No one noticed or spoke to me, maybe because I didn't know how to smoke cigarettes. When I went to the library and carefully walked up and down the aisles observing girls studying in their carrels, I was seeking some sign, some pinched mouth, that would indicate that another person felt the same pain as I did.

Because I repeatedly stayed late at the library and missed the bus to S.W. Atlanta during torrential storms and rumors of a White nurse being stabbed on Broad Street, my parents talked about my boarding at school, but not for the right reason.

As the first person to go to college in my family, I was trying to be both grateful and confident, the hard-working daughter who made her parents proud. Resolving to concentrate harder on my studies, I stopped wearing lipstick and cut Wednesday chapel. I took in hemming and button sewing in exchange for copying other girls' class notes, not because I cut any classes, but because when I reviewed my notes in the evening, I could not read them. After one or two lines of tiny, careful printing, the marks on the paper trailed off, dripping down, ending in gibberish. Every morning I vowed to be more careful, to sit up straight in class, to kick one foot with the other to rivet my attention, yet every evening I was alarmed to discover that my notes were worthless.

When I was not reading, I was picking at my skin. With a bobby pin I encircled every tiny pimple I could find on my face and pushed down hard until I resembled someone with the measles. To make sure all of my hair follicles were unimpacted, I twisted my head to see under my arms. While I read assignments, I clawed my scalp and examined the white wax and dried blood lodged under my nails.

At night my legs and arms itched; scratching raised a few irritated bumps that got infected. I squeezed them. Boils appeared on my ankles and inside my elbows. A carbuncle formed inside my left ankle. I eradicated it with an Exact-O blade, using hydrogen peroxide for medicine just like my grandmother did. When she poured it on my skinned knees, she would tell me to watch carefully until the pale dead soldiers came out who had valiantly fought the bad germs. The sores spread.

For months I was sick, but even my mother could not see under my long jumper and knee socks. What I could barely endure each day was the pain in my chest. The Pandora's box, with sharp edges that pushed against my lungs, stomach, and esophagus was trapped at the base of my throat, keeping me from coughing or speaking to anyone or laughing or sleeping. Finally, I went to the infirmary to say that I had a pain in my chest.

I was fascinated by the long gray hairs emerging from moles on Dr. Peters' face. She scheduled me for an upper G.I. Trusting she could make me well, I went home and fell into a relieved, relaxed deep sleep, with the fragrance of gardenia and honeysuckle in the air.

On the day of the test, I drank the barium, had the x-rays, and went to class. That afternoon the first sign appeared. In the restroom, I discovered that my excrement was white. With outspread arms, I told the first person I met that I was an angel.

The second sign of transfiguration appeared three days later when I awoke with a burning sensation. Across my waist was a wide scarlet area, already beginning to blister. A stigmata.

Dried blood marked my palm. With a pen, I drew a line to mark the sign. Abscissa. When the blister burst, I tied a cut up cotton slip from Granny's scraps around my rib cage for protection. No one could see my condition.

In this blessed state, my grades improved, but I couldn't write Greek philosophy and Old Testament and Hellenic art and French essays in a classroom full of other girls. Now that I had no physical boundaries, anyone's consciousness could merge with mine. Their sentences jumbled with mine. Their letters from home made me anxious. An eyelash in their eye scratched mine.

I needed to be alone, so I went to the infirmary again and showed Dr. Peters the sores on my leg and the now barely discernible burn across my waist. Antibiotics. Elevation of the limb.

Hot cloths for twenty minutes every four hours. Dr. Peters cut an X across my ankle and drained it. Her face didn't move as she made the incision.

I stopped riding the bus home. I was the only sleep-in patient in the orange brick building. My room had an adjustable bed, perfect for reading, one three-drawer chest and no mirrors, which was fine since God had finally taken my reflection from me to prevent my attachment to it.

The faculty left each day's assignment at the nurse's desk. My friend Jane brought popcorn. Alisoun and Harriet brought poetry and gossip. Dr. Peters brought the hot towels from a warming cabinet. Sometimes, the cloths were so hot they scalded the skin around the boils. I could feel the poison drawing to the center, the last vestiges of my fallen nature. When the doctor was out of the room, I pushed on the hurt places to hurry along the process of purification. Like Job, I knew that I was being tested.

People came to see me and told me that Dr. Peters did not have a reputation for cures. If she were a good doctor, they asked, why would she be content to work at a small college? Jane brought more popcorn, and we tested the phrase about "pouring salt on an open wound." Anna did not know what to do with my mother's messages; the dean's office only told them that I was safe. Dr. Peters had not notified my parents that I was locked in the infirmary either and that was fine with me.

After two weeks, my left leg stopped throbbing. A classmate from English class came to read "The Monk's Tale" in her Nashville accent and told me a theory that the accent, idioms, and structure of the Appalachian Mountain people, was a preserved form of Middle English. Alisoun said my leg smelled bad.

That evening, when Dr. Peters came with hot compresses, she screamed "green" and bounced her body down the hall to a telephone. An ambulance carried me to a local hospital. I was careful not to talk to anyone, to give out only my name and college major. Before sending me back to the college infirmary, they cauterized my ankle, leaving a crater.

I healed fast and stopped picking at my leg. If I got well, I might go to Jackson, Mississippi to see Miss Welty. I complained again to Dr. Peters about the box in my chest. Hiatal hernia she guessed and scheduled another upper G. I. and a lower G. I. as well. Government Issue, 1935. A thorough military inspection. Gastrointertestimonial.

On Friday afternoon when Dr. Peters left to deposit her paycheck, I hobbled to her office and read my chart. My eyes focused on the diagnosis: "Hysteria." Then, "Morning Enema." It was true that if I began to cry, I couldn't, of my own volition, stop. The tears were stored in the box, and came out of small cracks. Sometimes my hands and knees trembled so violently that I couldn't write or stand. I decided I was not going to have an enema, like my Granny used to give me from a big red rubber bag hanging over the bathtub. Somehow, I had to escape.

The lower G.I. was scheduled for the next morning, so I was not allowed any supper. In the evening, a student nurse was on duty at the front desk. There was no back door. A chant drove me in a circle inside my room: *Have to get out. Can't shout. Have to get out. When no one's about. Have to get out.*

At nine, climbing onto the sink in the bathroom, I was able to reach a window and unlatch it. Pulling myself up to the sill, I threw my body outside. People say "Pride goeth before a fall." so I carefully climbed down the bricks. Huddled behind a bush, I waited, catching my breath. I edged myself along the side of the building. When I reached the corner, I limped as fast as I could make my legs move to the hedge around the library and crouched there. In the darkness, I leaned against the cool stones to rest.

Soon the streetlamps cast a golden glow over the campus. Girls with their books strolled on the grass while friends paused to talk on the library steps and cluster under the ancient trees. The soccer team emerged noisily from late practice; dancers in leotards and wrap around skirts swirled to rehearsal in the auditorium. Sonatas and sarabands poured from basement practice rooms. From my vantage point, I could observe the world moving.

Feeling safe against the walls of the library, I needed neither food nor clothes nor shelter. I could command any book inside to reveal its contents to me. I would have no more library fines. No one would find me. I was safe. Forever. I was Amelia Earhart, protected by her plane's golden wings, pummeled to airy thinness. I had landed.

A bright light illuminated my head, casting a shadow on my lap. Had God come for me? I wasn't really ready. I needed to call my mother, so I was relieved to see that the light bearer had on big black shoes and khaki trousers.

"Come out of there, Miss. Get up." I could no longer command my body; it couldn't hear me. "You best come with me," he said, and I was glad that the security guard pulled me forward by the shoulders. He walked me to my bus stop and told me to report to the Dean's office first thing in the morning.

As soon as I reached school the next day, without stopping in the day student lounge, I sought out the dean, a short woman with a kind face. She had checked with all my professors and said I was doing well in English and Bible. I had some Incompletes in other classes and she thought I shouldn't put too many papers off until the summer. She said she was recommending to my parents that I be evaluated by a psychiatrist, and that if my parents could afford it, I might do better living on campus. She said it might be best if I first took a leave of absence from the college. I could say nothing but, "Thank you, ma'am, for seeing me."

The Family Physician

Our family physician was blind. He couldn't see the box in my chest that grew bigger, more painful every day, expanding from my throat down to my sternum, out to my ears. His stethoscope did not detect it. Did he know that my glasses would not focus? That fuzzy people followed me? That sidewalks undulated? Did he know God had selected me for this misery? *Did he know I was dying?*

I was weighed, measured, and tapped on the knees with a hammer. He drew blood to rule out anemia and thyroid problems. With a light, he looked in my ears, down my throat, into my gaze. Averting his eyes from my breasts, he listened to my heart. He did not ask me any questions. My mother said he was a Presbyterian Elder who never missed a Sunday. Those facts constituted infallibility. My bandaged ankle did not concern him because it was the responsibility of the doctor who treated it.

"Teenagers are a walking plague," he assured us, "always covered with fever blisters, acne, mouth ulcers, cuts, scrapes, insect bites. It's all those hamburgers and greasy French fries."

Yet I was a perfect physical specimen without any identifiable physical disease.

"I'm going to refer her to a psychiatrist, just to comply with the college requirements," he told them.

My mother looked shocked.

"I'll bet she has boy troubles," Dr. Needly smiled, patting me on the head and turning to my stepfather. "It may be just that simple."

"She fell down a hill once and hit her head," my stepfather offered hopefully.

Then I felt the shame. As they talked about me as if I weren't present, I grieved for slaves and livestock. With their backs to me, I heard Dr. Needly say, "...If you can swing it, Mr. and Mrs. Parent, I wouldn't turn this into your insurance company. Matters like this on your stepdaughter's record would keep her from being employed by a school system or the government..." It would be better, I thought, to have a brain tumor. Maybe I did have a tumor. A malignant brain tumor that had spread into my throat.

"A Jew," my mother said, looking at the name on the referral card. She wrinkled her brow.

"German Jew," the family doctor said. "Most of them are."

"Well, they're usually smart," my mother consoled herself.

On the way home, while they talked about taxes and what a fine Christian Dr. Needly was, I was elated that at last someone with brains would tell me why my body had a box inside of it. My mind was confused, and my perceptions seemed to have changed connections. I didn't even get angry that they kept the appointment card, and that I couldn't make my own appointment.

It would be eight weeks before I saw Jacob Occam, M.D.

Psychiatric Interview
with Spiders

The office was downtown in the same medical building as my ophthalmologist and the pediatrician who had prescribed leaving me alone to scream in the backyard to develop my lungs. The waiting room had the most recent copies of *Architectural Digest, National Geographic, The Saturday Review of Literature,* and *The New Yorker.* March and April 1963; May on its way.

Dr. Jacob Occam was impeccably dressed. His starched shirt cuffs showed evenly below his tailored coat sleeves no matter which way his arms moved. I sat down in a library chair, but he didn't ask about the weather or how I was feeling.

"Can you describe the events that precipitated your being sent to see me?" he asked.

...the precipitation most evenings is alarming in its duration. The Domino Effect: The spiders spread out on my eggs, I moved them out in the yard so they could go home, then they came after me. At school, the box lodged in my throat, God burned a mark across my stomach, and boils appeared on my leg. I was in the infirmary and escaped to the library. I kept quiet.

"How do you feel about being here?" he asked me.

"Happy," I replied, though "odd" first came to mind. *And how do* you *feel about being here, Doctor? Your face has a paucity of expression. Did they teach you that at school?* "Odd," I admitted.

"What's the earliest thing you remember?" He asked questions without raising his voice at the end of sentences.

"Having my tonsils out when I was five." I didn't know what was going to happen because no one told me where I was going. Later, they said I kicked the needle out of the nurse's hand.

"I remember the ether mask coming down on me." Unforgettable smell. Dots on the ceiling. Buzzing in my head. Dots smothering me. Fear. That was the beginning. ...*Crawford W. Long's magical gas. No, it wasn't the beginning...* It's only what I can remember as a unit.

"My mother bought me a bride doll and it fell out of bed on its head. It's a jolly good way to play dead, to fall out of bed on your head." *Do you like rhymes, doctor?* I was glad the doll fell because I was angry with my mother. *It makes presents suspect if you give them before surgery.* I was also sorry it happened and afraid she would be mad at me, so I stuffed cotton in the crack and kept the doll face up on my pillow pretending to love it.

Dr. Occam could read my mind. While I rocked back and forth holding my body together with my arms, that's what he was recording. My lips and jaws were stuck together, so it was better to breathe through my nose. Afterall, people had cilia for that.

"Would you like to go into a good hospital for a rest?" the doctor asked, smiling.

"Have you ever seen all of the Smithsonian?" I wondered aloud. That was where I wanted to go. In the hospital they might tie down my arms and legs to pass currents through my body. They would stop me from rambling, and I needed to hear myself or see my printed words to know what I was thinking. They might put me in a room without books or a typewriter. I had read that in Milledgeville State Hospital they put sixty people–the crazy, the retarded, the epileptic, the old, the abandoned, the down and out who are drunk–in iron beds, lined up and down the corridor, locking the doors. Even angels were stopped at the gates.

"I think a rest might be helpful to you."

"No!" I yelled. *I don't have time for that.* His face and eyes did not react. Did he hear me? *I will not go anywhere you send me because you don't like me! I am going to be your adversary even though I am afraid of you.*

"Tell me about destroying your room in high school," Dr. Occam said, writing in my file while I sat mute before his desk, not veneer, like our table at home that never had its leaves lifted.

His neck waited in its perfect collar as I studied the evidence on the mahogany slab between us. Onyx and brass paired fountain pens. His nails were buffed like his teeth, a distinct, quality of sub genus I'd never seen. I keep myself rocking and I can see that he writes the words "Blocking" and "Catatonic" on his pad. Between us in green jade, sits an early Chinese phallus on a pedestal, and a bust of Sigmund Freud without a doily underneath Freud's forehead is furrowed, and he has bags under his eyes. He has a beard and a bald head.

My mother always kills spiders, but I have been warned by Dr. Schweitzer not to. Judging Occam would judge this off the subject, I keep rocking back and forth.

Mama did not even flinch. Or wrap the bodies.

The news said more people were dying of cancer, and I presumed that I could help find the why. I needed growth hormones to introduce into cells, but my epistles so polite were not answered, so I was forced to make a crude substitution and inject bantam eggs with Vitamin A. I needed to watch my eggs through the night and keep the spacing and the temperature right. It was a house where stepfathers cut the power to keep me from reading late. It was a house where trays of eggs did not belong with schemes of violets and unused cups and saucers to be dusted. *God gave me the idea for my project.* I would not say that. That's a preservation rule.

"Tell me," Dr. Occam inquired, facing his diplomas. "Do you find spiders sexy in any way?"

He did not lean forward as if he wanted to hear what I might answer but leaned back against his cordovan leather chair with brass nail heads outlining the padded arms on which his long fingers drummed as if impatient for a response.

Why would I answer such a stupid question? I did not blink; I had to protect myself. He knew I had thrown shoes and books in my room at the ceiling. That I had gotten under the bed and refused to come out. My mother told him of those things, but not that she had slammed me across my ears with the upright Hoover vacuum as I ran from my bedroom.

I knew better than to tell them the reason why I had to hide; he wouldn't believe what I had so clearly seen when the daddy longlegs had come in the night, an army marching across the ceiling above my bed, to explore my room and look at me. While they each have but one pair of eyes, they can move their bodies in any direction. They do not spin webs and can play dead like a possum. I had watched one for hours on grandpa's farm, fascinated to see that it washed its legs by passing them one by one through its mouth. If a farmer loses his cow or mule and picks up a daddy longlegs by all of his legs except one, that one will point the way to the wayward animal.

"Do you refer," I burst, "to things about the act in which a species makes its babies, or do you mean the social and physical differences between males and females?"

"Which do you think I mean?" His writer poised, then wrote a prescription.

He didn't even know me, yet he prescribed Thorazine, little orange pills, one every four hours. And dropping out of school.

"I will tell you about spiders," I said. "Their long legs are the singed eyelashes of God."

Interior McCain Library, provided by Agnes Scott College Archives and Special Collections. Used by permission.

Bitch, There's Something Wrong with You

I don't know what prompted me to get up and leave the college library and turn away from the peaceful, golden glow cast by each lamp onto the girls' papers and books. I hoped that when some of them graduated, there might be a place for me at the tables. As I came down the front steps, I was surprised to see my boyfriend Alan at the end of the sidewalk. He carried a full schedule of classes at Emory University where he intended to go into law, so we only had dates on the weekends.

Behind him stood the towering brick Main Hall that once housed Decatur Female Seminary, one of the Seven Sister colleges of the South. Founded by the Presbyterians, the school was "to educate women for the betterment of their families and the elevation of their region." Although many boys in our accelerated classes did go north to MIT, Princeton, Yale, and Columbia, no girls from my high school went to college outside Georgia.

I had friends in this Gothic styled library although the girls studying in carrels never actually spoke to me, they looked up and smiled when I walked by. In the library I found dead men and women with interesting ideas, but when I included them in my essays, sometimes their words came back circled in red and marked "Tangential" or "Reference too dated." The library was funded by Andrew Carnegie who wanted to offer the same resources all over the country to rich and poor alike, but some places in the South, fearing they might be required to allow Black patrons, refused the richest man in the world's money.

Alan and I had gone steady all the way through high school. Because his family didn't have enough money, he was one of the few boys who didn't switch to a private school when the threat of integration began in the eighth grade. He invited me to every school dance: spring flings, bunny hops, and junior romps. All our dances were held in the school gym with parent and teacher chaperones circling the building in case Black kids might show up to crash our event. *Why would they want to*, I wondered?

Some of us joined a club run by parents called "Teen Cotillion" where we learned to waltz and tango, how to ask for the next dance, to excuse ourselves to go to the restroom, or to simply sit down. Some couples knew how to Jitterbug, but mostly we danced slow dances. Stepping to the right, then stepping to the left, yet always leaving a space between us through which light could shine, or so we were told. I was glad to be a girl because of how I felt when Alan's pelvis pushed against mine, hidden behind dampness.

Our school couldn't afford to hire a band so somebody's uncle played records into a mic, amplifying the skips and pops to songs like "Will You Love Me Tomorrow?" by the Shirelles, Roy Orbison's "Only the Lonely," and "Smoke Gets in Your Eyes" by the Platters. I liked "Save the Last Dance for Me" by the Drifters, but the big hit was a new dance called "The Twist" by Chubby Checker. To learn to dance to "The Twist," Alan and I swiveled our hips by twisting both feet as if putting out a cigarette on the floor while simultaneously bobbing up and down and leaning forward and back. Our youth group leader at church thought the hip movements were provocative, but once Chubby Checker was introduced by Dick Clark to screaming White teenage girls in high heels, there was no taking it back.

Alan despised churches because the women's foreign mission circles had not welcomed his mother when she became single. I invited him to my church's Christmas pageant every year, but even there, my stepfather never left us alone so as soon as Alan had a car we drove across town to the candle-lit Episcopalian church to hear "The Messiah." Afterwards we went to his grandmother's apartment in Buckhead when she was away traveling on senior tours where, among her many souvenirs and picture books from around the world, we could sit and talk privately.

For the senior prom, Alan had saved enough money from his job after school in a dry cleaners to buy me a black orchid. Because the other girls had corsages of pink carnations or white and yellow roses, I was embarrassed as the mysteriously delicate and graceful flower looked somehow evil.

"Don't dare touch it," Alan would warn the girls who came up to see it.

When I slipped on my coat as we left, the collar bent down the edge of one black petal, exposing its dark red flesh.

"Go in and get the flower box," Alan ordered me when we got back to my house.

I returned and held the box as he unpinned the flower from my strapless bodice. I held the box open as he carefully placed it back. Closing it, he put the box in the car.

"Oh," I said, thinking he wanted me to preserve it in the freezer.

"I'm going to give it to Mother," he said.

From the library steps, I recognized Alan's sloping shoulders and long arms that made him look to me like an ape. If my girlfriends saw this simian quality, they never said although they often pointed to his sandy, wavy hair, and sparkling blue eyes.

"We think they're so dreamy," they told me, and so did I.

He looked handsome in his ROTC uniform because it squared his shoulders. As editor of the 1962 high school annual, I had featured Allen's drill team and his company B of the ROTC. Except for flat feet and rheumatic fever as a kid, he would have gone to Vietnam upon graduation, even though he couldn't vote. To see awkward boys in Levi's, wearing uniforms and marching perfectly while twirling rifles with head turns was thrilling. What was the real point of appearing splendid on the football field only to scatter to the turf, roll away in the dirt, fire, and blow holes in the helmets of enemies when they had never before aimed at another human being? The boys had only read *Johnny Got His Gun*, about a World War I quadruple amputee without a face, and *Catch-22*, which came out our junior year.

On the battlefield, I thought that Alan would be a crazy man. I had seen his body tense, ready to spring through the windshield while driving when he talked about his father who had left him at age six and his waitress mother in her brown hairnet. His capacity for intense anger at his father scared me, filling my stomach with hot acid and knots. How could he be so gentle and loving toward me yet capable of such hatred?

I fell for Alan when, after an eighth grade Latin class, he came up to me in the hall and recited the declension: "hic, haec, hoc, huis, huis, huis." The sound was so beautiful that I fell in love. It was said that George Whitfield could make grown men weep by the way he uttered "Mesopotamia," so when we started passing notes to each other in class, I knew from his careful, beautiful scrolling script that he was in love. The sound of his love poems called attention to his rhymes and not to the subject, but what mattered was that he wrote them to me. He hand lettered "How

Do I Love Thee? Let Me Count the Ways." I kept all of his writing inside my pillowcase.

I loved Alan's high raised eyebrows that made me think he was always asking me "What?" because he wanted to know what I was thinking. And he listened. In classes, professors interrupted me before I reached my point because I prefaced my answers with, "This may not be true, I mean I'm sure there are other ways to look at it, but what if…?" Sometimes they asked me to repeat myself because my Southern drawl, passed down to me from people in English debtors' prisons who had been shipped to Georgia to serve as underlings to the aristocrats, was inferior to the accent of the girls from private schools in Virginia.

Finally, I developed a special language that I thought could be understood for any subject, be it Greek Philosophy, Old Testament Wisdom Literature, Botany, Piano, Beowulf and Chaucer, French, or Shakespeare. There was a procedure in class to speak. First, we were to raise our hand, but never wave it. Then we would wait until our last name was called. Once that happened, we could stand by our desks, leaving any scratched notes where near-sighted eyes like mine couldn't see them, and recite our answers. When it came my turn, I spoke.

"NoahveinedfortebathGilgasonnetdrowned," I said in what must have seemed like gibberish to the others.

My classmates snickered while the professor simply called on the next student. Eventually, I moved to the back row, kept my head down, and tried to speak only on paper.

Now Alan's sloping shoulders, as I took small wary steps forward, looked like the long-feathered wings of a dark messenger. He was not moving or flying towards me, only glaring; I wanted to turn away and run, yet I continued to move forward on the sidewalk, past the pretty white twin gazebos. I clearly heard a hiss. Then the word "Bitch." For some reason, I quickened my step to hear the word again. A female dog? My relatives said, "Son of a gun," but never "Son of a bitch." Women could bitch and moan, but they were not to be called bitches.

"So you had time for lunch in Decatur with Terry Hardman?" Alan said, as I drew closer.

"He was just on break from Yale," I tried to explain. "I wanted to hear what it was like going to school in the north."

"What did you two do?" he demanded. "Tell me."

"We talked," I answered.

"Unfaithful bitch!" he snarled. "After I've put up with you for so long."

When I looked down, I saw that the front of his jeans was flat. The special thing about Alan was that every time he saw me, his body responded in an erection.

"You're in another world," he said, shaking his head. "You can stare at God knows what on my dashboard or even in a restaurant for more than an hour. You're in another world," he repeated as he leaned forward, getting too close to my face. "I can't take it anymore," he lashed out, beating his arms against his jeans.

I often felt that I was only an observer, disembodied without any mind behind my eyes, yet I couldn't ask anyone I knew about this strange feeling. Day to day, I was simply frozen in fear.

"When I touch you now," Alan continued, "you freeze without blinking. Bitch, there is something wrong with you." And then the message the dark messenger had come to deliver: "I don't want to ever see or hear from you again. Got that?"

He opened his canvas satchel and pulled out a bundle of letters. I knew they were mine because I always decorated the envelopes with tiny, inked borders. His eyes were not soft but blazing.

"I no longer care about your poetic, descriptive gibberish," he said, "that you can't manage to say to me in person - like that you love me." His sulfurous breath singed the envelopes and ripped my words apart like an ape tearing through branches.

Turning away, I couldn't breathe. Trying to make my way back to the library, I stumbled several times, skinning my knees as if I were a child. He was still there. I could feel his eyes on my back.

For the next three days, I couldn't go to class for the pain in my throat and my inability to plan my next moves. I lost my school calendar. My bar of soap fell to the shower floor, so I got out quickly without wetting my hair. In bed, lying on my back, I made the sound of blinds coming down inside my ears so that the room was absolutely quiet except for the blood roaring in my head.

Blocking

D r. Occam added a drug called Stelazine to the Thorazine to treat what he called "Blocking," which I thought meant that I couldn't always tell him quickly the real source of my feelings, like I couldn't stand for anyone to touch me with rough, calloused hands because that reminded me of a man with fighting cocks who came to see my uncle and aunt when I was little. Dr. Occam never gave me time to answer his questions. The new Stelazine made me drowsy and dizzy if I turned around too fast, and my vision grew so blurred that I had to blink frequently to focus. I had trouble sleeping through the night and my feet swelled in my tight shoes. Dr. Occam continued to say I was still blocking, that I stared at something too long, and did not respond to his questions.

The word Blocking sounded to me as if I were interrupting him, playing loud music over his words, or putting out my leg to keep him from his office door. That wasn't the meaning, I learned. Blocking meant that he thought I was screening out all outside stimuli like a rat caught in uncertainty at an intersection in a B. F. Skinner maze. Human psychologists believed that in the presence of perceived danger, humans would automatically assume fight or flight behavior. Both of those reactions are observable. Perhaps the psychologists and behaviorists didn't know about an alternative reaction to danger, which is to freeze. By keeping absolutely still, you become invisible; no one can hurt you, or scream ugly words at you.

Since my ambition was to be editor of the *Aurora*, I got a summer job proofreading in the basement of the Retail Credit Company. I took the job because I would be working completely by myself while on Stelazine and Thorazine. The credit forms had print so small that a person applying for a loan would probably not read the fine print. Needing a job for the following summer, I signed up with Kelly Girl temporary employment services. Two days later I was called to go to an interview for the perfect job.

A book publisher downtown needed someone to type from written manuscripts on a big linotype machine. Sometimes I might also have to sit at the receptionist's desk when people were touring the three-story building. Some days I typed text for seven and a half hours. Sometimes I proofread long unnumbered galley sheets, marking up spacing mistakes. I couldn't understand why the boring stories I both typed and proofread were being made into books, except that they had bright covers. Every day I dressed up and wore high heels. The boss, Mr. Loveland from California, came downstairs most every day and told me what a great job I was doing and how much he appreciated my working for his company.

One morning before I left for work, my stepfather came to breakfast and flung the front page of the *Atlanta Constitution* across my grits. The headline, in the biggest lettering I had ever seen on a newspaper, said my boss had been arrested for pornography and three counts of sodomy. He was wanted in Los Angeles, CA. I read that he was a psychologist who had taped sessions with adults in swap clubs and open marriages, typed up the swingers' stories without permission, and published them. Some of his other books were on famous madams and brothels. The newspaper didn't explain about the charges of sodomy.

I had been proud that my name was listed as production staff of the Loveland Publishing. But now I couldn't put this job I was so proud of on my resume. Slowly, it dawned on me that I had not been hired for my typing speed. Following the dress code of my college, my arms were always covered, my legs were never bare, my neckline was discreet, I listened attentively, and said "Please" and "Thank you anyway," or "After you," because the last shall be first it says in the Bible. I was only hired for my appearance and manners, while I looked down on girls who traded on those superficial traits, accidents of birth, not personal accomplishments.

On a bulletin board at school, I saw tryouts posted for *The Summoning of Everyman*, a morality play written in Middle English. For the tryouts, we each read the same single page. I was selected to play Kindred and Good Deeds who goes to the grave with Everyman. Miss Winters was in charge of Blackfriars and her assistant was Miss Green who had a green room where we put on our costumes. The dry mouth from my anti-psychotic medications made it hard to always say my lines so I carried mints in my pockets.

Miss Green blocked out our movements on stage. Careful blocking would allow everyone's lines to be heard. It was important not to have your back to the audience or to be behind a taller person. Turning slightly instead of being front on was the best angle to deliver lines. When others had lines, it was important for you to think about where you were in the frame and to react to what was happening. Even exiting should be planned.

I started to block everything I had to do that was stressful. If there was a talk or an exam in a strange classroom, I went to the room ahead of time and felt how it was to be in the space, looked at where the windows and doors were, selected where I needed to sit. I wouldn't get lost and be late because I had already been there.

When I climbed the stairs to the second floor in Buttrick Hall, on my way to recite Keats' "When I Have Fears That I May Cease to Be" in the tiny office of my teacher, I felt as if I might pass out. My heart beat too slow and my leg muscles were heavy as cement blocks. Unable to walk straight, I fell against Professor Preston's desk. My eyes were yellow. The hospital said my 8 mg. dose of Stelazine was too high and that I had Stelazine poisoning.

I could not understand why Dr. Occam had not informed me of the side effects of either Thorazine or Stelazine, and which ones would signal a medical emergency. Didn't it matter that I was in college? The story I submitted to *Aurora*, "Can I Go with You?," was about not being told I was to have my tonsils taken out in a hospital and then being blamed for fighting against the nursing staff. It was essential for me to know ahead of time what was about to happen.

~

I had to go home for a week. On the weekend we visited Uncle Judson who had ulcers and Aunt Willadeen. The treatment for ulcers in the stomach was drinking whole milk, even tablespoons of cream. No matter what complaints my uncle made about pain, his wife would say, without going to the kitchen, "There's some milk in the icebox." That sentence played over and over in my head until it stood for bad communications, expectations, a tragic past, and misplaced blame between a husband and wife. I knew how to type it up in a drama format from scripts I had used. Miss Trotter had me send it to *Mademoiselle's* College One

Act Play contest, won the previous years by Arthur Kopit and Edna O'Brien. My play won first place. They sent me the galleys to proof, and I irritated the editor by presuming to send them a layout for the first page. They informed me that their Art Director was handling the presentation. They also wanted to know the source of the curtain line, "Oh, Lord, that's the showing forth," but I could not remember.

Blackfriars collaborated with the Arts Council and actors from Emory University and Georgia Tech to stage the play in the new Dana Fine Arts Building with Miss Green as the Director. The milk carton in the icebox spoiled, making the actors gag, while the poor grammar written for the wife in the play considerably bothered the English majors.

Miss Trotter sent my play to Paul Engle and asked me to write him about the summer session in creative writing at the University of Iowa. Paul Engle was the first student to ever present a work of the imagination as a graduate thesis. I sent him some stories from a group called "Suffering the Things." He wrote back to say that he would accept me in the Iowa Writers' Workshop Master's program the following fall, which would mean I would leave my college without an undergraduate degree. Even Miss Trotter thought that was risky. I didn't venture mentioning the possibility to my parents.

I threw myself into theater and reading plays. In the spring, Blackfriars was going to stage *Blithe Spirit*, by Noël Coward. I played the carefree and outgoing Elvira Condomine who, in death, socializes with Genghis Khan. Elvira was practically opposite of my temperament, but I had my lines and good blocking by Miss Green. The lead character, Elvira's husband, is an author who hires a medium to perform a seance from which he hopes to get ideas for his next book. My ideas always came from real people.

My favorite play and the last one in which I had a part was Samuel Beckett's *Waiting for Godot*. I played Vladimir, one of the tramps who keeps waiting with Estragon for Godot. The dialogues, at the end of both acts, summed up my life with so many supportive people urging me forward as a writer, yet I didn't know how to block out that life.

Estragon: *Let's go.*

Vladimir: *We can't.*

Aurora, Digital Collage from author's photos of *Aurora.*
By Elizabeth Shepley, 2022.

Aurora

The bus from my house reached the campus early. No one was in the day student room, so I went to the college self-service bookstore next to the mail room where I had put in a job application. The pack of 3 by 5 note cards I needed was next to envelopes and Peanuts holiday cards. When I went to pay, I saw a stack of glossy paper booklets on the counter that were free. It was the Spring 1962 issue of an Arts Magazine for Student Expression called *Aurora*.

I liked the name "Aurora" because language does bombard the atmosphere of the mind with charged particles. I had never seen the green shimmering lights of an aurora borealis because Atlanta's sky had too many commercial lights. The first beautiful lights I remember were from Mrs. Hitchcock's Sunday school class. Twenty of us had flashlights put through a hole in a white paper plate and we sang, *"This little light of mine, I'm gonna let it shine."* Then we marched around the dark sanctuary singing, *"Everywhere I go, I'm gonna make it shine."* When I closed my eyes tight at night, I saw bright colors inside my eyelids. Candlelight services in church were solemn and beautiful, but we carried those tiny candles on white paper circles for Good Friday before the crucifixion and also on Christmas Eve, when we sang "Silent Night." The Alpha and Omega.

The northern and southern lights with their trembling curtains of red, blue, green, and mystery, were thought by the Vikings to be a reflection from the shields of the Valkyrie maidens who take dead warriors to Valhalla. Slaves and farmers who lacked a sword or an axe could not go there.

I took a copy from the bookstore with me to read. Inside was a three canto poem by Mary Womack called "The Rape of the Dempster-Dumpster," inspired by construction work behind the college dining hall. There was also a one-act play, stories, poetry, watercolors, sketches, and essays. I looked to find a faculty member's name for submissions, but the journal seemed to be edited, printed, and published by students. I needed to contact the student staff. I thought I might do that.

I was taking freshman English from Dr. Pondergast who had us for the first two months write five paragraph essays. The first paragraph had to say what I was going to tell readers, while the second through fourth paragraphs were supposed to say what I wanted to say. Finally, the last paragraph would restate what I had told them that I said I was going to tell them, which meant that I had made up my mind. Hard as I tried, I could not manage to write the five-paragraph essay as I thought that the main point should build to the end. If the words in each paragraph led me forward, how could I know ahead of time where the words wanted to go? On the bus and at home I wrote poems instead of prose from rhythms in my head.

One morning when I reached the campus as Hiram Washington was making the rounds of unlocking doors, I went to Dr. Pondergast's office and slid my poems, "Mercy" and "Margaret," under her door. Her first name was Margaret, the same as the famous anthropologist who clutched her little purse in front of her lap when she spoke to our student body, but the inspiration for my poem came from Gerard Manly Hopkins and his sprung rhythm poem "Margaret, Are You Grieving?" In my poem Margaret answers. It was the first time I felt calm and hopeful at the same time. I had seen that the words left after my crossed-out fragments could be reworked. Experience was salvageable. The path leading to my first class did not shift under my feet.

I took creative writing in place of French again, as an independent study, with Dr. Margaret Trotter. She was from Virginia, had been published in *The Saturday Evening Post,* and had graduated from Wellesley, Columbia University, and Ohio State University. She had come to the college the year I was born.

Dr. Trotter had me read Chekhov and Flannery O'Connor.

"Tell me, what did you learn?" she asked, looking up over her glasses at me; her thick, wiry, almost black eyebrows lilted up with her questions, almost touching her fluffy white hair. One lesson from Chekhov was that "If a gun is on the fireplace mantle in the first act, it must go off in the third." Otherwise, why waste the words describing that gun and distracting the reader?

"Remember, Miss Henderson," she consistently told me, "the whole truth is never believable." Emily Dickinson said to "tell all the truth, but tell it slant." Is there a story not being told? In the third week, when she asked me to write a family story and read it aloud, I uttered some dialogue that sounded completely unnatural.

"Listen to people as they talk on the bus and in the dining hall," she instructed me, "and to your mother on the phone as she talks to her best friend. Observe how people interrupt one another and write down on your cards what you hear."

She urged me to be curious about every "fact" I thought was true. For other assignments, if I looked up every interesting word and the social and political history behind the setting in an academic paper, I would get a very low grade for not observing the page length assigned, but writing a story was different. Instead of pointing out all the less than perfect parts of my stories and word choices, Dr. Trotter would tell me what she liked, what worked.

"If this didn't have value," she would say, pointing to a place on the page, "I wouldn't insist that you work on it some more." From her I learned that I never needed "just," "very," or "so." My attention span while taking Thorazine was long enough for writing poems in one sitting but not enough to finish pieces of prose. It was difficult for me to sit still with my restless legs wanting to spring up.

The first story I wrote with Dr. Trotter, "Saturday Morning," was about a third grader's first friend who is pulled out of school by her missionary parents. After more than a month of editing I submitted that story to the *Aurora* for the Fall 1963 edition and it was accepted. I received a note in my mailbox from Frances, the editor. A lanky girl from North Carolina whose parents were both lawyers, she answered every question I asked her over lunch until she had explained all the procedures from handling submissions to printing and distribution.

Students I did not know told me they had read my story and remembered how big people trivialized little people's love of their first friend and their pet. I did not have to say the first words of greeting, which I was not very good at doing. I could share a story with girls across the campus, girls in higher grades, from Kenya and Kalamazoo, whom I might never meet in person, all because of text on the pages of *Aurora*. I was invited to join the freshman writing group, Folio. Membership was by try out and so was being included in BOZ, after the pen name Charles Dickens called himself. When I got to be an upper classman, if accepted, I could meet in the evening at Miss Preston's house with other student writers to read our work.

I became a boarding student my sophomore year and moved my coffee pot and dictionary to the Publications house to do my schoolwork. There I could participate in the discussions about upcoming issues of the *Aurora*. I had a story or poem in every issue. In the Fall of 1964, I featured the work of five artists and wrote about the technique of Scratchboard Designs.

One week, someone told me that the ground floor room of Rebekah Hall had red walls. As soon as I saw it, I imagined hanging an art exhibit there, followed by an art auction, and holding weekly poetry and fiction readings. I called the event the Inferno and members of the new Arts Council and *Aurora* helped make it a success.

I went to Hoke Smith Technical School in Atlanta in the summer to take Proofreading and Editing. Then I was chosen Editor of *Aurora* for my Junior and Senior years. In 1966, Pendulum Book Projects printed the Spring issue, expanded from 28 to 78 pages. That issue included the complete bibliography of Ellen Douglass Leyburn, chair of our English Department. Her first publications had been poems in *Aurora* in 1927.

In the magazine, I added an essay by Theodore Meyer Greene to student work and papers that student philosophy and literature majors had presented at conferences. At the end of my junior year I wrote a long, detailed exegesis of the use of the color and word "green" in *Portrait of the Artist as a Young Man.* I also won First Place from *Mademoiselle* magazine for a one act play. Ellen Stoianoff from *Mademoiselle* wrote to tell me that my short story had also won first honorable mention and to ask me for more samples of my poetry.

At my college, I could take Directed Writing one year and an Independent Study for a writing project the next. However, Miss Trotter thought I could use more intense study, but undergraduates were not eligible to attend the Bread Loaf School of English. I was also too young for the summer program at Converse College. To enter the Iowa Writers' Workshop Master's program the following fall, I would have to leave Agnes Scott without an undergraduate degree.

In October of my senior year, I received a letter from Judith Jones, Editor at Alfred A. Knopf, who had been forwarded my winning one act play by the Fiction and Poetry Editor of *Mademoiselle*. She said that my writing was "frighteningly observed," and asked, that when I had a long work of fiction, that I let her see it, but as I hadn't finished my collection, I didn't write back.

At first, I thought I would put together some stories and call them "Disrememberings" until I came across the word "lexicon" in the poetry of Denise Levertov. My planned chapters would be separate stories with titles in alphabetical order: Apple, Aurora, Bad, Before, Choice, Christmas, Doctors, Finale, Fire, Gwine, Honor, Justice, Kindred, Last, Legacy, Lucid, Menses, Neuro, News Paper, Offence, Oratory, Pretend, Quiet, Respect, Temp, Tiptoe, Transit, Understanding, Virgin, Visible, Vocabulary, Water, Waver, Xmas, Xobliterate, and Yoke. I would call the novel *The Candace Lexicon* after the narrator, Candace Lee Jackson.

But what Candace could not do was write a letter to her Granny Henderson who was in a retirement home in east Atlanta. It would be easy to drop the cover of her winning play into an envelope and address it to her grandmother. Were there words to lace together the world of Candace's home with Granny and the new world of Women of Letters?

Give Me Oil in My Lamp, Keep It Burning

In the fall of 1965, the English Department put out a call for submissions to be sent to the Southern Literary Festival in Mississippi to be held the following April. I submitted "The Cut Sashes." Two seniors, Frances and Susan, asked me to go with them to the Mississippi State College for Women in Columbus, Mississippi.

I told my parents that my English class had to make a field trip to Mississippi, and they gave me the Greyhound bus fare. I told them my psychiatrist Dr. Occam thought it would be good for me to go, but he didn't. He thought people were happiest when they stuck to the same routine every day. I called his message service to remind him that I would be missing my appointment.

"Please hold," the secretary said, surprising me, "Dr. Occam would like to speak to you." What was it, I wanted to know, astonished that he would talk to me when he wasn't being paid to do so.

"Miss Henderson, I have a favor to ask of you," Dr. Occam began. "I need you to promise me that if ever an idea popped into your mind to do anything that might, even *might*, harm yourself or anyone else, you will please wait twenty-four hours."

"Certainly, Dr. Occam," I readily agreed, having never considered doing either.

I had never been out of Georgia except for riding the *Nancy Hanks* train once to see Mama's sister in West Palm Beach and a summer car trip when there was a flood in Louisiana. The only thing I knew about Mississippi is that out of the 50 states, it was always at the bottom in wages, money spent on education, healthcare, and civil rights. But I also knew that William Faulkner, Eudora Welty, Richard Wright, Shelby Foote, and Tennessee Williams were raised there.

The weekend I went home before my trip, I ransacked the closet for my red beret. Finding it, I next tied a string around my forehead and carefully trimmed my bangs. Placing the beret on my head, I stuffed the jagged edges of the sides and back under it. I listened patiently to my mother tell me my beret would be hot on the bus, but I didn't care.

~

We stopped for a rest break at a Greyhound station next to a Holiday Inn. Susan had heard that labor unions were trying to get contracts in all southern hotel chains.

"Daddy says that if the Blacks don't like it, the unions will bring in the Cubans," she said, taking a drag from her cigarette.

I knew that in Atlanta, Scripto employed Black women, at better wages than they could make cleaning the houses of White women, to make ink pens, mechanical pencils, and cigarette lighters. Even so, when the company refused to recognize their union, 700 women took to the streets to protest. When Martin Luther King, Jr. took up their cause, the company begrudgingly gave the workers a Christmas bonus and four cent an hour raises to show them that they didn't need to organize. The public-school teachers in Atlanta were also trying to form a union so administrators would pay attention to their needs in the classroom.

"Honey," chimed Susan, "I wouldn't bother my head thinking about people I don't know in the first place." I liked Susan because she was deadly honest.

I don't know why I was always making rhetorical speeches on the stage of my cerebrum. The bus passed mile after mile of shacks and ragged clothes hung out to dry. I hung my messages on a clothesline strung across the temporal lobes where informa-tion from the outside world was coming in at all times.

It was to Susan and Frances that I tried out the idea of form-ing an Arts Council to coordinate student programs in painting, sculpture, drama, dance, poetics and to promote art exhibitions. The college had a Christian Association, an Athletics Board, an Honor Council and Martyr Board. How could a liberal arts col-lege not also have an Arts Council?

"Because," said Susan, "the college has never had one and everyone there has been there forever, and they believe only in slight changes every century or so."

I studied the problem. How could I get the faculty to pay attention to me other than to watch me from out of the corner of their eyes for strange behavior? I needed others to go to the faculty. How was I going to garner enough friends to support my idea? I would have to learn to smoke cigarettes.

Smoking. I needed to learn to smoke. The popular students did not study in their rooms, but in the basement or upstairs in the Hub with the smokers. Sometimes, professors would come into the Hub to smoke and discuss things with their favor-ite young scholars. I was willing to discount the fact that I was asthmatic, that I had never seen any of my Methodist relatives smoke, and that my mother said smoking would turn my fingers yellow. In addition, my body was the "Temple of the Holy Ghost," not to be defiled.

When we stopped for lunch in Tupelo, I watched Frances light up, saw how she shook the match six times after it was out, which fingers to hold the tube with, how long to hold the smoke in the back of the throat before blowing it out. There was a proper angle to the head for exhaling that directed the smoke away from the person in front and at the same time managed to call attention to the activity.

"I must have dropped my cigarettes on the bus," I said, as I fumbled in my pocketbook. "May I steal one of yours?"

Frances cracked the pack on the edge of the table causing a cigarette to spill forward. She offered me a light and I put the cigarette to my lips and sucked in. I had heard stories all my life about fathers breaking little boys of trying cigarettes by making them inhale until they grew nauseous. I rolled the smoke to the back of my throat, and nothing happened. I blew the smoke out and inhaled again. It was easy.

Smoking made me feel alert and sophisticated. I got change for a dollar and bought my own pack of Winston cigarettes from the machine. By the time we arrived in Columbus, I had finished that pack and bought another. I was a fast learner.

Smoking gave me something to do with my hands and a reason to stand at some distance from people with whom I was engaged in conversation. Smoking enabled me to pause between sentences to consider what I might next say. Smokers didn't have to smile.

When we arrived in Columbus and found the registration table, there were cut glass ashtrays next to the sign-in sheets. The lawn outside was studded with many girls in their summer dresses.

We slept in the dorm that night, and I stayed up long past the other girls, smoking as I read and re-edited "The Cut Sashes" in case I was called upon to read it. The memory of a song I had learned in Vacation Bible School accompanied me.

Give me oil in my lamp, keep it burning.
Give me oil in my lamp, I pray.
Give me oil in my lamp, keep me burning
Keep me burning till the break of day.

The next morning, we went to a memorial service for John Crowe Ransom's wife. The color scheme was coordinated with pink roses and cherry-pecan cookies. The book editor for the Memphis Commercial Appeal talked about recent releases by Southern writers and the soprano Miss Lucille Haney sang. An announcement was made about Flannery O'Connor's health. Hudson Strode spoke of Thomas Wolfe and his editor wrestling with three thousand pages. Paul Engle from the University of Iowa read and criticized poetry. I had taken a second place for a small lyric about sea birds. Ruth Gordon and Garson Kanin appeared for questions two hours before they were scheduled to read the winning works. He had a gold loop in one ear.

I had a red beret.

In the late afternoon we listened to a panel discussion on Historical Writing and Folklore.

In the evening John Crowe Ransom, Rhodes Scholar, leader of the Vanderbilt "fugitives," founder of the *Kenyon Review*, critic and poet, was the keynote speaker. At seventy-five years old, he was still a groomer of both style and imagery. I stood in a line to get his autograph, but when he asked my name, I was unable to say.

"Are you deaf?" he shouted at me.

I went outside to walk around. When I returned, the glow of fifty tapers illuminated the banquet table through a haze of smoke. Strong coffee and bourbon from silver flasks, carried in the inside jacket pockets of gentlemen of letters, mulled together in heavy china cups. I was looking for Miss Eudora Welty; people said she sometimes stayed away from big noisy to-dos and they accepted that. Men and women waited on one another for extra coffee, spiced pecans, and fresh napkins. The head table seemed to shift around the hall. I thought of my Little Granny and her daughters, always serving the men, always at their beck and call.

"Is Truman Capote here," I asked the woman next to me.

"Just because Truman apes Faulkner in wearing a white linen suit, does not mean he is one of us," she scorned. "He spends most of his time in New York City."

"What about Richard Wright?" I had read *Native Son*.

"Honey, he might have been raised here, but he's a Communist, doncha know?" I asked if she had read Ralph Ellison's *Invisible Man*?"

"He may be named after Emerson, but he's a Communist too."

"Maybe it's like James Baldwin says, nobody knows his name."

"I heard he's light in the loafers," she smiled. "A nervous Nellie, you know."

In search of a restroom, down the wall-papered hall with Georgian moldings, I saw the kitchen, steam coming out the door. Inside, four Black women with their heads wrapped in scarves were stuffing dates, spicing roasted pecans, and rolling up crab balls.

"The food y'all are making sure is good," I said.

"Sure putting it down fast, honey."

Returning, I lingered in the doorway, my wobbly legs unwilling to take me back into the banquet hall. With Thorazine, I couldn't drink any alcohol or safely pour coffee into another's cup. I wanted to crawl under the linen cloths with the polished shoes and listen to the conversations. I had to scream at myself to keep my knees from bending down. In the shadows a familiar voice whispered, "You're not going to make it, are you?" I clung to the doorway and said, "Shut up."

Fortunately, Susan appeared. "Honey, did you forget where your seat was?"

"I have trouble seeing in the dark," I told her, feeling grateful.

After midnight, Peter Taylor was persuaded to recite one of his short stories and to comment on entries. He read out loud two of my sentences. I was astounded. They stood stronger than I. He had supportive comments for each fledgling writer and shared some of his own failures. This was surely the banquet spoken of in the New Testament. Almost.

At the table I pulled one of the note cards out of my purse and wrote down what was on my mind to say. Trembling inside, but going ahead, I said to the six people at my round table, "Y'all notice there aren't any Black writers, editors, or writing teachers here."

"Maybe they just didn't want to participate."

"Lawd," the woman with the grey bun on the other side of me enjoined, "we've never heard a bunch of them tell about us. Won't that be the day!"

Yes, it would.

I had to sort over tables stacked with fresh and worn penned and typed manuscripts to find mine. I had conversations to overhear and people to watch. Suggestions to make. I had to learn what Granny did not teach me, and that was how to know when not to put the same effort into a costume as a winter coat. To recognize the difference. Everyone knew my Granny's perfect stitching; no one knew her.

I needed more note cards. I needed real friends. When I was older and could do it, I needed to actually talk to my mother. I needed to grow up. I needed to find out for what God intended to hold me accountable. I had work ahead of me, and it was for me joyous. By vigilance I had been counted with the Wise Virgins. I would not be left wandering dark streets searching for oil, lost without maps, stepping over puddles.

Melodies, Methodists, and Morons

The organ was already playing a prelude when the ushers led us to the front two rows, the only available pews in the packed sanctuary of Audubon Forest Methodist Church. The choir, in long green robes with white V neck satin collars, entered filling up one row after another. Most of them had silver beehives or French twists, while the men had shining bald heads. In front there were two rows of teenagers, mostly girls. Since we didn't have time to get programs, we were going to watch the singers and organist without knowing the name of the pieces or who the soloists were.

I had never seen Rev. Bevel Jones, but I had heard about him because he was one of the organizers of 80 ministers who had signed a Manifesto Against Intolerance. My Presbyterian church and the Baptists were planning to move outside of Atlanta because of school desegregation. Nobody said anything, but everybody knew that was the reason. Rev. Jones' Methodist church did not have a Christian and an American flag on each side of the altar.

His opening prayer was short, asking for blessing on the choir's singing and our hearing. Rev. Jones then turned and joined the tenors on the back row. When the lights dimmed, the sanctuary became completely quiet.

A teenager on the front row, in the same green robe as the others, stepped forward to the lectern. He had closely cropped red hair, sort of a big nose, freckles on his forehead and cheeks, some pink splotches of acne, and dark eyes that looked out at the audience. I thought he was going to sing, but without looking down at any open text, he began to recite verses from the Book of Revelation.

"And I, John, saw a new heaven and a new earth, for the first heaven and the first earth had passed away, and the sea no longer existed. And I saw the holy city, the new Jerusalem, coming down out of heaven from God." As he spoke, I thought, *All the visions I knew from the Bible were of prophets and angels and Christ ascending into Heaven with Sputnik.* "And I heard a loud voice from the throne say, 'See, the home of God is among mortals and God himself will be with them.'" *Wow!* I thought. *That last book in the Bible, which I had never read, was all about predicting disasters. This was different.* The boy lowered his voice and slowed his cadence as he read the voice from the throne so that we in the congregation had to listen closely.

"'He will wipe every tear from their eyes. To the thirsty He will give water as a gift from the spring of the water of life.'" I thought in amazement, *I could not even imagine God down on earth or up above paying attention to my tears.* "'Death will be no more,'" he intoned, "'mourning and crying and pain will be no more, for the first things have passed away. I am the Alpha and the Omega, the beginning, and the end.'"

At the end of the sentence about a Holy City on earth, not up on a hill or in the clouds, the speaker bowed his head so that I could only see his ginger, cinnamon hair. *A strange thing to do,* I thought. *Was he reading what was next? Was he thinking about the words he had read to me?* He raised his head, and I thought he looked directly at me and continued with his velvet voice.

"'See, I am making all things new.'"

I turned and whispered in my friend Carolyn's ear, "Who is that? Do you know?"

"I think he's the President of their youth group," she shrugged. "That's what someone said."

"He has a beautiful voice, don't you think." I exclaimed.

"I bet he never shuts up," she said, and I didn't reply. I was enraptured and I didn't even know his name.

When the concert was over, I saw some choir members talking to people in the back pews, so I approached and asked who the reader was. "Why, that's Sid," they said.

Although Frank never gave me the time of day in our Presbyterian youth group, because he had always liked my sister who was now dating someone else, he called to ask if I would go on a double date with him to see a production of *Othello* downtown. Othello was to be played by a White actor while the rest of the cast would be Black. I would never pass up an opportunity to see a live play, so I immediately said yes without asking with whom we were going.

When he came to the door that Friday night, a blue Studebaker idled in the driveway with a red head at the wheel. Frank and I slipped into the back seat. The girl in the passenger's seat with shoulder length blonde hair, turned her head, and said her name was Tabitha Green. I could remember her name from the gobs of green iridescent eye shadow that caused her to blink so slowly that it appeared she was falling asleep. Frank introduced the driver as Sid. Immediately he started singing *"Trouble, We Got Trouble, Right Here in River City"* from *The Music Man*. He sounded exactly like Professor Harry Hill, complete with hand motions over the steering wheel. I knew that voice.

All the way through the play at The Academy Theater, Shakespeare's lines were obscured by whispering Tabitha Green. Sid had his arm around her shoulders and Frank tried to do the same to mine, but I leaned forward as if I needed to hear better.

On the way home, Frank wanted to neck in the back seat even though he didn't even like me. Instead, I bent forward over the back of the front seat to talk with Sid. I learned that he was a Methodist like my mother's relatives. Of course, I knew all about John Wesley, who brought Methodism to Georgia, and his brother Charles, the composer of 6,500 hymns. There is nothing more inspiring than hundreds of people standing to sing "O for a Thousand Tongues to Sing."

"My father likes to sing 'Life Is Like a Mountain Railroad,' but I don't think any Wesley wrote that one because everyone likes it."

"I never heard of it," I said. "I bet it's not a hymn."

"It has a refrain." he said, and I could hear the smile in his voice.

"A song about trains wouldn't be in our hymnal."

"I wonder how many different hymnals there are in the world," he poked at me. "Just listen to this," he said. "This was written by Charlie Tillman in Atlanta."

The Studebaker lurched forward, passing cars in the next lane. *"Watch the curves, the fills, the tunnels, never falter, never fail,"* he sang above the roar of the engine. *"Keep your hand upon the throttle, and your eye upon the rail."*

"Slow down," I yelled from the back seat, "or you'll kill us all!"

"Christ, woman, your voice could make me wreck!"

So, I shut up. Sid eased up on the gas, and we rode in silence for a while, except for the sound of Tabitha sniffling.

Then, breaking the tense silence he announced, "I don't believe I'm really a Methodist."

"What do you mean?" I asked. I was still a Presbyterian whether I liked it or not, but I had visited the Unitarian Church twice.

Sid was silent. Then he announced that "There's no Supreme Being with a long beard and a flowing robe resting on a cloud, watching for everyone on earth to break some rule written a thousand years ago."

I agreed. "That would take a million pairs of eyes."

"I'm connected to everything and every person alive on this planet and all the stars in the Universe, too," he said.

"You mean like an infinite string of Christmas lights?"

"Exactly. Except the tree is so big we can't see the base or the top."

I was stunned by this image, but then I had to be a smart aleck. *Did he worship the first mover or creative spirit in all things?* I wondered but did not ask. Instead, I said, "There's a word for that kind of belief, but I can't remember what it is."

"Does that mean I am not allowed to think it?"

"Of course not," I replied, but before I could say more, he broke into the old North Carolina murder ballad "Tom Dooley." How could his mind shift from a serious religious discussion to a mere popular song? Sid knew all the verses, and after we heard the chorus, we all joined in, even Tabitha. When we reached my house, Frank did not even walk me to the door or say he had a good time.

It was eleven o'clock and my stepfather was waiting, as usual, at the door. I went straight to my room, closed the door, and turned out the lights until I thought he might be asleep on the other side of the house. Finding my flashlight, I pulled a blank postcard from my desk.

In teensy writing at the top left, I printed my address. Consulting Miriam Webster's red dictionary, I wrote that arrogant Sid the correct definition of pantheism. For good measure, I added the definition of theism, deism, dualism, and variations by Spinoza and Goethe. Feigning humility, I wrote, "I have seen it a million times but must have never learned it." To be friendly, I added at the bottom, "No wonder we couldn't think of it," which made no sense because it implied we were doing something together. I signed the card "Happy Butterflies, Bonnie Jo" and affixed a five-cent stamp.

Although I didn't write my phone number on the postcard, I silently waited a week for Sid to call, knowing he could look up my number with the address and last name. When he didn't call the following month, or the next, or the next, I tried to forget he ever existed.

In my junior year in college, I was finally making good grades and had become president of the Arts Council. In the Spring, I got a call from down the hall. No one ever called except my mama on Sundays. The student who answered the phone said it was some guy named Sid.

Without saying hello he asked "Will you go with me to my fraternity's party at the lake?"

We were discouraged from going to fraternity parties at Georgia Tech, and there was the added hassle of having to sign out and back in at Main Hall, but beyond that, I couldn't think of an excuse not to go so I said, yes. Not knowing what to wear, I asked my friends who took me down to Casual Corner in the Decatur Square and helped me pick out some Bermuda shorts, which I didn't like because my knees were ugly.

The party itself was memorable for the fraternity brothers stomping about and shouting around kegs of beer and running about like morons. Looking down, and not up at where I was going, I bounced off the broad, naked back of a brother and stumbled into Sid who easily steadied me. I could hardly tell one from the other with their crewcuts, wide shoulders, and tanned bodies, yet Sid could as he apologized with an easy smile to the boy he called Bill. Sid didn't seem like the other brothers at all with his pale skin and baby blue tee shirt.

"They only let me in because I raise their grade point average," he shrugged as Bill lumbered off towards the lake. "I don't think they really like me."

Down by the lake, we watched as one brother, with an insolent grin on his face and a can of shaving cream, would run up to a girl, pull out her bathing suit top, and squirt shaving cream down the front of it. Almost immediately behind him, another crewcut, tanned hunk would throw her into the lake. Since I didn't bring a bathing suit, I stayed away from the mayhem.

It seemed that everyone but Sid and I got drunk and more or less staggered to their cars or passed out. Instead, we found a relatively quiet spot under a pine to lay out the blanket we had brought for a picnic and looked up at the stars. I was going to be late to check back into the dorm, but I wanted to stay I guess I was surprised that Sid did not defend or apologize for the behavior of his frat brothers. While I don't think he approved, he seemed to tolerate them the way they were. Lying on the blanket, his hands folded behind his head, he began to softly sing and hum, *"It Takes a Worried Man to Sing a Worried Song."* I loved his melodious voice as much as the first time I heard it. As we gazed up at the stars, with the pulsating glow of the lightning bugs dancing above our heads, the world felt new. I decided then that Sid would be a good person with whom to leave home.

Milk of Paradise

If you really want to know why I, as well as Harriet and Jane, each the junior stars of the English Department, took an Incomplete in Romantic Poetry, you need to understand what it was like to have been invited to Alisoun's Elfin Grot on the night before final exams. Whether or not there was a full moon, I don't remember, but that dorm room was full of passion and rage and pleasant pain.

The invitations, hand lettered, were pushed gently under our doors on Thursday morning: "Come into my Elfin Grot/and there we'll eat and sign full sore /And there we'll shut our wild, tired eyes /Just we four." Signed, Alisoun. There were instructions to "R.S.V.P. by noon/meet at dusk, 'neath the moon." With exams the following morning, none of us really wanted to leave the library for an encounter with Alisoun's eccentricities, but we knew how sensitive she was.

Alisoun, born to middle aged parents, was an only child and spoiled rotten. From her rambling old house in the hills above Chattanooga, Tennessee, Alisoun's mother had written letters to women's clubs, begged and borrowed from the bank, and sold her mother's cherry wood furniture and Old Master's silver to accumulate enough money to send Alisoun to the best liberal arts college for women in the South. Alisoun was a fine enough student, but socially she was shunned. She did not own a black dress or pearls and was not a member of Daughters of the

Confederacy. She was endomorphic and wore baggy, flowered cotton dresses her mother made.

From the time we four took Chaucer together, she considered herself the reincarnate Wife of Bath. She was gat-toothed with hammer toes that prevented her from squeezing into stylish loafers, and her mouse brown hair hung down her back in strings without waves or curls, the result of an old Southern family intermarrying, it was thought, until physical qualities and character declined. Having an amorous nature, Alisoun spoke of herself as lusty. When she got out of bed with her books, which was seldom, and came to class, she would make sweet moans when moved by the professor's explication of a passage. A sign over her bed quoted Keats in his letter to Benjamin Bailey— "O for a life of sensation rather than of thoughts."

As darkness, like veiled melancholy, fell over the college, we left our library carrels and walked to Alisoun's dorm where she had a room in the tower. Harriet, who Alisoun called Cristobel, brought her leotards and ballerina slippers since she was practicing with the dance troupe. Jane, called by Alisoun the Darke Ladie, brought her scissors because she never passed up an opportunity to make extra money by cutting hair. Alisoun's name for me was Psyche.

This Elfin Grot was dark, lit only by candles. We shuffled slowly through all the clothes, underwear, and towels covering the hardwood floor. The stereo was playing Chopin piano concertos. Alisoun was wearing the navy men's raincoat that was lately her uniform in winter over her thin dresses. The room smelled of gardenias, hyacinths, roses, and orange peelings. Alisoun frequently went out at night and raided the botany garden. Almost everything she really enjoyed was against school rules.

Whenever the girls received food from home, they were called care packages, but those from Alisoun's mother were something else. At the center of the buffet spread on Alisoun's mattress was a sliced Smithfield ham. A brown earthenware pot contained baked beans with sorghum syrup and red pepper pods. There were jars of brandied peaches, green tomato pickles, and pickled watermelon rind with crushed ginger. A basket of chicken crackling biscuits with huckleberry muffins sat alongside. On Alisoun's dresser, damson plum caramel pie and white fruit cake with citrus, coconut, and almonds awaited. She had a jug of dandelion wine on the floor and another container labeled, "Milk of Paradise."

Alisoun purred from the corner as we filled our paper plates and sat cross-legged on the floor. We spoke of Professor Preston's latest lecture in which she said that poetry speaks anew with each reading. She was a short, stubby, unmarried woman who privately published her own volume of verse called *Upon Our Pulses*. Her students showed respect for her elegantly structured lectures and hated her guts.

Stalking around the room, Alisoun began to recite "The Rime of the Ancient Mariner." She knew all seven sections by heart. Each damsel in Professor Preston's class had to memorize a poem and recite it with feeling in her office. Most students selected sonnets or short odes. Alisoun always did everything in excess or didn't do anything at all.

"Beware! Beware her flashing eyes, her floating hair," pointed Cristobel. She danced in little circles around our bulky friend.

"Show us your esemplastic powers," called out the Dark Ladie.

Alisoun, continuing to recite, opened her raincoat for all to see that she was completely naked. Her broad, soft flanks were as white as a bridal gown.

"I have been fucked," she said.

"By whom?"

"By Professor Preston. She gave me an F on my Keats essay because I didn't follow directions." We were to write two pages on some aspect of the poet's letters, and most had made A's. "I wanted to trace Keats' conception of the Temple of Delight in his letters and poetry, and I read all the commentaries of Sidney Colvin, J. M. Murray, Ridley, Matthew Arnold, Swinburne, and Arthur Symons. It came to 15 pages, and I couldn't cut a single word."

Feeling slightly smug, we comforted her. Harriet said Professor Preston would probably drop the lowest grade. With her mouth full of green tomato pickles, Jane said Alisoun should go to the Dean. Alisoun said she felt no relief in woe, that her chances of getting into graduate school at Stanford, and leaving the South for good, had evaporated. We demurred. Surely that wasn't so. She had to keep trying, but in our hearts we knew the Dean would never change the grade of a full professor who was at least 60 years old, and we also knew that a lifetime could be charged because of one failing grade. Cristobel said the academic establishment was not supposed to teach them what to think, or how long to think, but how to think. We agreed that what Professor Preston probably didn't like was that Alisoun had read all the critics instead of confronting the original source.

Alisoun nodded in the shadows. "I took strange love and read it deep. I lived and breathed the primary sources. Anyway, where would Professor Preston be without centuries of criticism on her subject?" Alisoun sounded angry but in the candlelight, we saw tears streaming down her round face.

As Alisoun proceeded to waive her Keats paper through the candle fire, she grabbed up the jug of dandelion wine and poured it on the flames, which leaped higher. The amber liquid drenched Alisoun's trench coat and fell on her men's loafers. Jane filled a shoe with water to pour on the fire, then refilled it. Harriet turned an entire container of honeysuckle-scented body powder upside down on the dying flames. Alisoun recited Southey's "My Days Among the Dead are Passed." Compelled to cheer up our friend, Harriet, as Cristobel, proposed that Alisoun have her hair cut, and Jane, the Darke Ladie, agreed.

We pulled Alisoun to the floor, where inertia kept her down. Cristobel gave her a neck massage, and the Dark Ladie began to brush out the long, matted locks.

"Tonsure me," demanded Alisoun. We protested, but she was determined. A wide quietness saturated the room as Cristobal wiped the blades of her scissors. First, she cut off about 10 inches of Alisoun's locks, then parted off a forehead section and cut it to within a half inch of Alisoun's scalp before trimming the rest level with Alisoun's ears.

"Close your eyes to keep the trimmings out," Cristobal requested.

"With holy dread," Alisoun complied. The Dark Ladie, growing leaden-eyed staggered to the dresser to find a mirror for Alisoun to see herself. "Fair dame am I," Alisoun incanted. "I need a garland."

We found a bra on the floor and fastened it around Alisoun's head. She beamed. Her cheeks turned a faded rose. She pulled herself up by the bedpost and went to the window and shook the old wooden frame to open it.

"The first person to hear a cock in the night singing 'to whit, to who,' can have some Milk of Paradise." We feigned listening, and said we heard it, although the only sound from outside came from crickets in the hedge below.

"Conversation is not a search after knowledge, but an endeavor at effect," Alisoun recited, claiming that Keats wrote that to Haydon in 1819, and that she had figured it out in 1965 but was going to keep it a secret. She gathered our paper cups and poured in the milk. It tasted like eggnog with a lot of nutmeg. It was so delicious that we drank it all, believing that so doing would prevent us from getting hungry during the night while cramming.

We had some more pie, talked about taking Shakespeare and Fiction of the Forties together next year and, one by one, fell asleep on the piles of clothes and hair. Maybe we heard Alisoun say "Adieu! Adieu!" when she left; maybe she said nothing. She was apprehended the next morning in the botanical gardens wearing only her raincoat, smelling of alcohol, and "palely loitering." She was expelled from the college.

We slept peacefully through the night and woke up too late to take the Romantic Poetry exam. Like Isolde, when she came too late, we grieved. Professor Preston would not allow us to make up the exam, and we three had to repeat the course the following year, to graduate a year late. We received one letter from Alisoun postmarked Los Angeles, proposing an answer to Chaucer's Knight's search to learn the thing that women love most. It was "verse, fame, and beauty." Keats had the answer.

"Darklings," she wrote, "I listen with soft-conched ear for your voices. Have mercy on my soul."

We did not write back.

Another Incomplete

Last night I tried to dream
about Hamlet in my closet or quail eggs gray blue.
Raccoons stood in my window wondering
could the books and notes in my bed be food?
I didn't dream about buildings with tunnels
but final exams in a grey locked room.
My dream catcher is cobwebs.

Dreams want an able-souled citizen,
require work be done before bed, not in it.
I was disarranged between blankets and blouses.
My alarm was in my shoe, my socks stuck in my ears.
I didn't withdraw from my day soon enough.
Now I have to endure the night,
which sends me another Incomplete.

So Happy Together, Digital Collage from author's photos.
By Elizabeth Shepley, 2022.

The Best People

We both had fresh undergraduate degrees and tearful parents. Sid was due to report for work in New Orleans at AT&T Long Lines to be trained to make proposals to companies looking to update their communication systems. I planned to use my English literature degree to find a summer job typing, copywriting, and greeting with a smile. We departed Atlanta with two loaves of banana bread from my mother and two hundred dollars from Sid's father for a first and last month's rent.

Sid and I were married on June 13, 1966, the day after I graduated. Somehow during the ceremony, we managed to keep perfectly straight faces as the congregation stood and sang all eight verses of "Come Thou Fount of Every Blessing." For a month the organist had refused, claiming our hymn wasn't appropriate. *Oh, but it was*, to us. Our favorite line was "Here I raise my Ebenezer/ Hither by Thy help I've come." The organist tried to insist we sing Wesley's "Love Divine, All Loves Excelling," which made human love seem somehow paltry. Then, out from behind the maroon altar curtains, after what I thought had to be the pause before our vows, came the pudgy tenor from our chancel choir singing "How Great Thou Art." I knew full well that my Mama was behind this. To her thoughts, everyone who admired the Rev. Billy Graham also loved George Beverly Shea's rendition, and so, they would love my wedding. Mama knew I couldn't protest, so when she helped me change clothes in the Wedding Parlor after the ceremony, I remained silent, but as soon as we could leave,

Sid and I fled the Presbyterian reception, without any spiked punch, let alone dancing, in the Adult Always Faithful Sunday School Room. Our car was already packed.

By dusk we were in south Georgia, passing stands with pecan pralines, watermelon, and hanging coconut heads. It felt good to leave home, to anticipate an interesting new job in New Orleans, and to learn to live with a new husband. As we drove along a dark stretch of highway, Sid slowed down as the road narrowed to one lane. We heard singing and laughing and felt hard whacks to the back of our Studebaker Lark, but we could see no one. Sid turned down "It's a Hard Days' Night" on the radio, then off. We sensed people standing to each side of the car Sid's mother had given us, so Sid slowed down some more.

"Keep going," I said, "but stay steady."

Inching forward, we saw nothing in the headlights and only shadows in the rear-view mirror. Why weren't there streetlights? I had heard stories of Black folks driving through small White towns after dark, getting pulled from their cars, beaten, their automobiles set afire. Surely no one would do that to us. I realized that no one knew where we were, but we were nice, and we were White. Besides, if they knew us, how could anyone hate Sid and me?

Still feeling a little shaky and tired, in the next town Sid pulled up to a hotel that was older but hopefully cheaper than the new turquoise and aluminum motels everywhere. I hoped it would have antique furniture. The inside smelled like my Mama's basement. The cheapest room turned out to be on the third floor at the end of the hall with EXIT on the door. Sid fell on the bed in his clothes, and I went to the sink to wash my face and take out my contacts I had gotten a week before the wedding. Without being able to see the yellowed sink clearly under the dirty bulb hanging over the bed, I missed the tiny white cups trying to put the hard plastic lenses to bed. The right one I thought was still stuck to the end of my index finger, fell down the drain. My "Oh, no" woke Sid up. Straightening his clothes, he tried the phone, and then ran downstairs since no one answered at the desk. A few minutes later, he returned with the hotel's dark-skinned, grey-haired handyman who probably had the skills to do anything, but shook his head at the problem.

"These pipes been rusted a mighty long time," he said, taking a wire brush to the rusted joint. "Can't take apart anything to fix in the hotel nowadays unless somebody wants to replace 'um, and I can tell you: they don't."

Sid, who thought he could take apart anything and make it work better, stomped around the room in anger at the old plumbing or maybe with me for being so clumsy. Either way, I was relieved because those contact lenses hurt every time I blinked. Truthfully, I loved the glasses I had worn since fourth grade.

Arriving in New Orleans late the next afternoon, we stopped at a chain restaurant I loved because of the bread. Instead of biscuits or cornbread, the table had a basket of delicious, glistening yeast rolls, brushed with butter. When we finished our catfish, slaw, and French fries, the Black waitress came to clear our plates. As she moved to take away the basket, I put my hand out to stop hers, asking her to leave them because I really loved those rolls.

"You're not from around here, are you?" she asked.

"No," I said, "we're from Atlanta."

"You can't get a roll after I've done touched them," she told us.

"Who says?" I wanted to know, but she didn't reply. Instead, she brought me a new basket of bread without adding it to our bill.

After three days of looking, we found an affordable apartment on the second floor of an 1880's Queen Anne house in the Garden District. At a distance, the street was beautiful, with gingerbread Victorian houses and French cottages next to Greek revival antebellum mansions. The gardens were full of azaleas and roses beneath crepe myrtles and arches of live oaks. Within a week, we found that the lushness was tempered by spiders, beetles of every description, buck moth caterpillars that stung, and creepy cockroaches.

The landlady, Miss Abbie, had divided the house into four apartments. A young couple with a shiny red Mustang rented the ground floor apartment next to hers. In the apartment next to ours lived Miss Crowley who had handled our lease arrangements.

Our apartment was not air conditioned, and the open window breeze left what felt like drops of warm rain on our arms, faces, and backs. Perspiration continually dripped down the sides of our glasses. My blouse and Sid's shirt stuck to our backs. We fanned our necks and underarms with two matching funeral parlor fans imprinted with, "I will not leave you comfortless." The clammy cotton sheets clung to our skin.

In the tall French closets of the furnished apartment, with its small wallpapered sitting room and larger bedroom, hung striped, grey silk dressing robes on brass hooks. The kitchen, with crusted black grease in the oven that I was afraid would catch fire, must have been a hallway before the house was divided up. During the day, I kept the back porch door open for ventilation; at night, cockroaches scurried across the clothesline where I hung Sid's shirts to drip dry.

Hoping to cool off one night at the end of our first week, we ventured down the creaky stairs to the front porch where the landlady, Miss Abbie, and her companion, Miss Crowley, spent every evening in their green rattan rocking chairs. Their chins were tilted up. Once seated, on the steps, we also looked up. As our eyes adjusted to the light against the lavender sky, we saw rats crawling back and forth across the telephone lines like spies in black jump suits patrolling the roof of a building. When I looked back down, Palmetto bugs were playing chase on Sid's loafers. He quickly got up.

"I can't stay here," he said. Sid was terrified of bugs. I accepted his squeamishness around insects and spiders because I valued the lovable tenderness that kept him from stomping them or ever cursing anyone who did. I adored him, and he knew it. The women glared up at us as we stood.

"It's a beautiful evening," I said.

"I reckon y'all settled in," the landlady uttered as if it were a question to which she didn't care about the answer.

After a few days of suffocating heat, we decided to cut down on our grocery budget and rent an air conditioner that Sid would install himself. Returning with the heavy box, he said he was almost unable to rent the unit.

"The manager wanted to know where I was from and if I were baptized!" he exclaimed. "So, I told him I had been sprinkled." Sid handed me the man's business card with his home address and phone number on the back. "He says we need to be baptized by immersion to be saved. And he has a swimming pool."

Two days after Sid installed the air conditioning unit, we were summoned to Miss Abbie's quarters at 8 pm. The invitation was in script on a yellowed calling card. We finished our frozen spaghetti dinners, brushed our teeth, and headed down the worn green carpeted stairs. Downstairs Miss Crowley received us. The room was dark and full of vines that trailed over and around family pictures and candle sticks on the mantel before circling the lamps. Three cats snoozed on the brocade white couch. In the corner, on a large chintz-covered chair with an elaborate crocheted antimacassar on the back, sat Miss Abbie. She had a large lap, evident even in her navy crepe dress with a cameo pin on the collar. Her white hair had a wiry permanent wave that parted over her pink scalp. Her pink bedroom slippers had tiny rosebuds across the vamp. A long hair grew from the black mole on her left cheek, and the table lamp next to her cast a shadow shaped like the leg of a spider. Neither woman shooed the cats off the couch, so while Miss Abbie looked us over as if we were stray dogs of uncertain pedigree, we settled down among the cats.

"Y'all just have a seat and I'll heat up the coffee," Miss Crowley said. "I perked it this morning." I had visions of being force fed black tar. When I was a kid, my Mama told me that drinking coffee would turn my knees black, so of course I started drinking the coffee in the bottom of adult's cups, the same way I put my mouth on the separate water fountains so I could see if it would give me a baby, or simply to prove that my relatives and teachers at church and school lied all the time.

I told Miss Abbie that she had a lovely parlor.

"Well bless your heart," she said without a smile.

Sid noticed the framed portrait of Jefferson Davis over Miss Abbie's chair and elbowed me. Did our landlady even know that Lyndon Baines Johnson was now President of the United States? Miss Crowley returned bearing a silver tray with saucers and cups half full, sugar cubes, heavy cream, and a cookie tin with a bent lid.

"Thank you so much," I said while Sid said nothing.

"I don't see you going out much," Miss Crowley observed. "The Duchamps go out whenever he can come home early. He's an intern at the county hospital, you know."

"No, I didn't know that," I said. "We like to read to each other in the evening. J. R. R. Tolkien."

"Oh, my goodness," Miss Crowley exclaimed. Gazing at me sideways, she said she supposed I was a true Georgia Peach.

"Georgia *is* called the peach state," I corrected her. "But that's not a nice thing to call any lady," I said in a louder voice than I intended.

When I was eight years old, I thought people were remarking on my rosy cheeks, but by the time I was 18 I had learned that Georgia Peach meant that a woman had a nice plump, firm butt, fuzz, and juicy insides. After I explained that, I immediately knew I had been rude, but Miss Crowley quickly changed the subject by telling me that Miss Abbie wanted to know what part of Atlanta we lived in?

"What part of Atlanta, dear?" Miss Abbie echoed.

"Cascade Heights in Southwest Atlanta," I replied.

"Then I don't suppose you attended that excellent school, Westminster, on the northeast side?" she inquired.

"No ma'am, I went to public school."

"Well, what exactly does your father do?"

"He was an accountant for a steel company where he met my mother," I informed her. "Then he went back to college for an MBA and DBA."

"Business? What kind did he own?" she asked, perking up.

"None. Actually, he's my stepfather," I replied. "My real father painted murals and portraits."

Miss Abbie's mouth dropped open and her face seemed to stare into an abyss.

"And what about your father, young man?" she asked, turning her attention to Sid.

"He's a trial attorney," Sid told her, eying his coffee cup.

Miss Abbie smiled. "And you studied the law of course?"

"No, I didn't," Sid said. "Dad handled homicides for the Black community plus a lot of divorces to make money. We always had weepy women at our house that my mother had to listen to and feed, phone calls at all hours, and angry husbands showing up with guns wanting to kill my father."

"My, my, I wouldn't have put up with that. Perhaps if he had represented a better class of people." The old lady was quite spry when she shared an opinion.

"I majored in electrical engineering," Sid told her.

"I guess we do need those...to keep our lights on," Miss Abbie conceded. "Bill Duchamp's father is head of internal medicine at Baton Rouge. Bill has a great future ahead of him."

"He's lucky," I said.

"His wife has already joined The Junior League," Miss Abbie claimed, "and the Garden Club."

"Some women have to work," Miss Crowley said softly. She was a short woman with no waist and bobbed hair. I wondered how long she had functioned as Miss Abbie's caretaker or companion.

As if Miss Crowley heard my thoughts, she told us, "My mother was Miss Abbie's mother's housekeeper, in this very house."

Miss Abbie shifted her weight with labored breathing. "My people go back four generations to the settlement of New Orleans," she said. Her eyes closed. Then she suddenly leaned forward. "Tell me. What did your people do in the War?" The D. H. Holmes personnel manager had asked me the exact same question before he offered me the Executive Secretary job in

Contract Renovation and Decorating. What did it have to do with anything?

"My great, great grandfather fought in the War," I recalled, "but he left the battlefield to go back home to his farm. He'd heard that the Union army had burned his smokehouse and wounded his only milk cow. And his wife was pregnant."

"He was a deserter then?" she asked, eying me over the rim of her cup.

I saw no use in responding.

"But surely *you* are still a member of the United Daughters of the Confederacy?"

"I don't think so," I told her.

"I have a framed certificate in my mother's basement from the Sons of Confederate Veterans," Sid interjected. "It says that a Private Augustus Schell died of the measles in his first month of service. My mother's grandfather almost starved to death in a prison in New York. But after the surrender, he walked all the way back to East Point, GA. Mother still has the single Confederate dollar he put in the sole of his shoe."

"What was his rank?" Miss Abbie questioned.

"I have no idea."

"Well, I declare."

Sid and I had planned to get our college diplomas framed when we had the money and hang those, not pictures of dead, tragically deluded heroes. We would not want to inherit the large portrait of Robert E. Lee that Sid's father displayed prominently in his office.

"We'd better go," I said, stroking the gray cat next to me. "We have to get up early."

"Oh, my heavens," exclaimed Miss Abbie.

On the stairs Sid put his arm around my shoulder. "How'd you like the inquisition?

"I'm in shock, I guess," I confessed.

"Well, I don't like anybody treating me as if I'm beneath them for stupid, prejudiced reasons."

Inside, the air conditioner hummed. The perspiration that had coated our foreheads on the way up the stairs began to dry.

~~

Sid was getting ready to take a bath in the claw-foot tub when the doorbell rang. Wearing a towel and grabbing the grey dressing gown that came with the bedroom, he opened the door a few inches. It was Miss Crowley.

"Miss Abbie forgot something important she needed to tell you," Sid opened the door further, but Miss Crowley backed up in the hall. "Your air conditioner is dripping on the Duchamp's unit, and they're afraid it's going to rust the housing."

"I'm sure the water on their air conditioner is only condensation," Sid told her.

"The Duchamp's *own* their unit, and it does not drip," Miss Crowley informed us. "Maybe your rental unit is defective."

"Miss Crowley, there are rat droppings in the bottom of our closet and under the sink," I said over Sid's shoulder, "and cockroaches on the porch."

"Well, don't worry if you smash one, "she said. "They clean up after us and themselves. Did you know cockroaches eat their dead?"

"No, I didn't," I admitted, feeling sick at the thought of it.

"Well, your air conditioner is the first thing," she said. "And the other thing is that Miss Abbie doesn't think it proper to leave your underwear hanging on the back porch in broad daylight."

I moved to the door. "No one can see the upstairs porch over the tall bushes unless they are looking on purpose."

"It just won't do for y'all to have an air conditioner upstairs. 'Nuf said," She concluded.

"But it's unbearably hot up here," I explained.

"You see what you can do," Miss Crowley said, backing away. We thought she was leaving, but she returned and poked her head in. "If you can't do something about the dripping water and the underwear, this may not be the best situation for you. Of course, we wouldn't hold you to your lease."

We were stunned. With both of us working every day, looking for another furnished apartment would be impossible. And we had committed on paper to renting the air conditioner for three months. The worst part was that I was sure that these problems would have been overlooked if we were descendants of some important old Southern family with sons who had gone to West Point and distinguished themselves in battle and lost their legs. While we *also* were from old Southern families, our old Southern families had descended from hard working farmers who had been shipped from English debtors' prison to the Georgia colony where Oglethorpe wouldn't allow slaves, aristocrats, or Catholics.

Both of the tall windows in the parlor were as high as Sid could raise them while the fan on the AC unit circulated the air. Outside, a mockingbird sang after another bird warbled its night tune, and an owl in the background punctuated the dark with a questioning contralto, "*Who? Who?*" Were we who we thought we were?

"Maybe we should move, Sid," I said. "I don't feel welcome here. They don't like us."

"Look, this isn't a social gathering or a communion table," he said. "I don't really care if I am welcome. I just want the right, same as anybody else, to live where I please."

"Come here," I said as I went to close the back door off the kitchen. "You can hear them."

"Who?"

"The roaches on the clothesline," I said. "Listen. Their legs make a noise and so do their smacking mouths."

"You're imagining things."

"Just listen, will you?"

"They're disgusting," he shivered.

"Try pretending they're highwire artists in the circus," I suggested.

"And who would pay to watch them on our porch?"

"It's all in your point of view," I said. "Maybe they only need a striped tent."

"And maybe all we need is a new car and our very own air conditioner," Sid said and paused. "If we only were related to some Confederate officer who held back General Sherman from taking Kennesaw Mountain and marching into Atlanta."

"What we *need* is to go live somewhere else."

"Hell, we have a lease," Sid said, his face turning red to nearly match his hair. "And we haven't broken the terms of that lease." He dropped down onto the bed and its springs squeaked in protest.

"No, I'm not talking about this buggy apartment, and that old fashion, mean spirited landlady. I'm talking about leaving the South," I clarified, surprised to find that my arms were raised up over my head like a holy-roller in a shout.

"What?" he pulled up to sit on the edge of the bed. "We can't do that," he said, shaking his head. "We can't do that to our families."

"Why not? Our families are both out of touch with what matters to us," I said. "They think that if you go to church every Sunday, God will bless you with a house, children, and good fortune no matter how you treat other people."

Sid was silent. "The problem is that other parts of the country look down on people from here. You know that. To them, we're beer drinking, gun toting Neanderthals with a blonde on our arm who can twirl batons while singing *Ave Maria* and stirring up a pound cake."

"And have beautiful babies," I nodded. "I know what you mean, but I'm certainly not a Southern Belle."

"Well, what do you want to be?" he asked.

"I don't know," I said. "I only know I do not want to live *here* or any place like it. And I do not want to be a teacher with the best bulletin boards. I don't think I can tell the nice stories about our history."

"I can't really make my parents proud by getting a job for IBM and wearing a blue suit and tie every day until I die."

"So you are giving up on being a 'Scion of the Southland,' dear?" I smiled.

"Never," he declared and mockingly stood, hand over his heart, to sing part of the Georgia Tech Alma Mater. "*A brotherhood in praise and song, in memory of the days gone by, oh, Scion of the Southland, in our hearts you shall forever fly.*"

In silence we sat side by side on the end of the bed attempting together to imagine a life beyond these regional confines, yet unable to clearly know what might lay ahead.

On Saturday morning Sid bought some plastic pipe and tape to redirect the drip from our air conditioner down onto a geranium. He also bought 25 feet of clothesline for me to string across the sitting room. We decided that one of us would also get up at six to go outside to wipe off the top of the Duchamp's air conditioner.

Over the next two months, the complaints seemed to stop, but when we passed the intern outside getting into his car to go to the hospital, he managed to look past us, to never make eye contact. His wife would only nod at us on the stairs as she brought up crisply ironed shirts from the dry cleaners. I would rather she stuck her tongue out at me than treat me as invisible.

The last week in July I was called into my boss' office. I had written him a memo after I discovered that the Board of our firm was always selecting the bids for renovation jobs from people whom they had previously worked with or their relatives.

"Listen up, honey, we aren't paying you to think," he said, "and we aren't paying you to write down what *you* think either. Thank goodness you're going back to Georgia in September." A Southern gentleman would not have added that last remark.

The president and vice president of Tony Scarpelli Plumbing and Services were killed in a car accident the night before Sid was to make his sales presentation. Sid was actually relieved. This company, which was the most popular and the most profitable in the city of New Orleans, had moveable ropes between departments from which the orders were fastened using clothes pins. The new telephone equipment would have cost them $4,000.

Despondent, Sid put off making a report to the Atlanta office that he had failed with his first sale. Although he wasn't let go, he didn't go back to work. Instead, he answered ads from life insurance companies like New York Life and the one promising the buyer a piece of the rock. While his interviews were successful, he had to take aptitude tests, revealing that he might be good in many fields, but he should never, ever try to sell anything.

Soon he found a job at Radio Shack where he didn't have to really sell anything but only find what the customer already knew he wanted. Plus, he got free copies of *Popular Mechanics* with news about fledgling data storage companies for personal computers. That first week in August, I asked him to go get his shirts from the back porch.

"You do it," he said, running back. "There's a giant roach on the line."

On the back porch in broad daylight, I met a two-inch-long roach. When I was a thumb's length from her front leg, she began to back up, her eyes with their thousand lenses staring at me, the porch, the ceiling, and the floor all at once. Her chocolate mouth moved from side to side. The spiracles on the sides of her body moved as she breathed. The antennae rose and she darted at me. I knocked her to the floor and started to crunch her. But I couldn't. Grabbing Sid's shirts, I shook them, and ran back to hang them on the inside clothesline. Sid asked if I had killed the roach.

"No," I stammered, "I couldn't. Her relatives were here long before Miss Abbie's."

The next morning, I went out to the porch to check the weather. At first, I thought the cockroaches were gone, but then I glimpsed the edges of their brown wings and saw that they had flattened their bodies to fit between the green floorboards. I envied their skill at protecting themselves.

Before I could put on my blue sheath dress and high heels, Miss Crowley pounded on the door.

"Gary Duchamp was late for hospital rounds because he had to wipe off his air conditioner. Your cheap unit is leaking again."

"That's his problem," Sid answered. "Everything in this climate sweats. Maybe you need new downstairs tenants who complain less."

"Why, the best people love it here," she exclaimed, taking a step back.

"Well, we don't," said Sid. "We've decided to cut the summer short and leave at the end of the month." I had a job to go to at Rich's Department Store in September, copywriting for a Hail Britannia campaign promoting British goods. I hoped Sid would go to graduate school where he could take the new computer science courses. He'd have to get a job too because we would need to pay back my teaching scholarship from the State of Georgia.

"Leaving early, kids? Pray tell," Miss Crowley said. "Oh to be young and full of false hope." Throwing up her right hand, she waved as she turned and walked towards the stairs.

"Let's go," Sid said, with his arm around my shoulder.

And I said, "We can."

Acknowledgements

Jen Harris, my consummate editor, who shared my curiosity on the origins of Southern sayings. She might suggest that every fact I stuck in as essential might not be, but always waited until I could see that for myself.

Elizabeth Shepley, artist, author, and creative living coach, created the collage graphics in this book and prepared the electronic manuscript, while gently asking me how my timeline was progressing.

Casey Westerman, College Archivist and Librarian, McCain Library, Agnes Scott College, Decatur, GA., a gifted sleuth who could sort through the rich history of the college and root out 1962-66.

A special thanks for the faithful and inspired teachers of the writing craft whose workshops and classes I have been fortunate to attend: Dr. Margaret Trotter of Agnes Scott College; June Shillabeer at Everywoman's Village; Celine Marie Pascale and her Wordshops for individuals with serious mental illness; Roz Spafford of UCSC; Page Stegner who told me my fiction was "a tied up dog"; Raymond Zager who came bearing journals for everyone; Nina Hart who introduced me to Magical Realism; Katey Schultz who advised me to Revise! Revise!; and Jessica Lowell Mason and Janelle Cagnon who taught the Herstory method of visioning a disturbing moment.

To my friends, who helped me say "No" to interruptions and joining committees: Mary, Betty, Alison, Martha, Eric, Sandy, Anna, and the Chock Full of Nuts girls.

And to my daughters, Hannah and Elizabeth, ever my inspiration finding their vocations, who respected Mama's project and work schedule.

About the Author

After 30 years in California, where Bonnie Schell founded a drop-in center for people experiencing madness, and frequently homeless, she came home to the South. Her memories are now included in the anthologies What Does It Mean to be White in America?: A Collection of Personal Narratives, The Unbroken Circle: Stories of Cultural Diversity in the South, and in WNC Woman. Her poetry has been featured in Coastlines: Six Santa Cruz Poets and in Knut House Press: The Insanity Edition. Diagnosed with schizophrenia at the age of 17, Bonnie was later co-editor of On Our Own Together: Peer Programs for People with Mental Illness and Reaching Across with the Arts: A Self-Help Manual for Mental Health Consumers. Raised in Atlanta, Georgia, on Vacation Bible School songs, Separate and Unequal, potlikker, and the King James Bible, she lives in Asheville, NC, with her big Russian Blue cat, Smokie.

You can find out more at bonnieschellauthor.com.